MM

KT-445-032

happy
toddler

gentle solutions to tantrums, night waking, potty training and more

DR REBECCA CHICOT

Vermilion

1 3 5 7 9 10 8 6 4 2

Vermilion, an imprint of Ebury Publishing,
20 Vauxhall Bridge Road,
London SW1V 2SA

Vermilion is part of the Penguin Random House group of companies
whose addresses can be found at global.penguinrandomhouse.com

Penguin
Random House
UK

Toddler yoga illustrations © Stephen Dew 2015

Chapter opener illustrations © Katie Saunders 2015

Permission to quote from *Raising Blaize* by Debra Ginsberg,
© 2002, has been kindly granted by the author herself

First published by Vermilion in 2015

www.eburypublishing.co.uk

A CIP catalogue record for this book is available from the British Library

ISBN 9781785040108

Printed and bound in Great Britain by Clays Ltd, St Ives PLC

MIX
Paper from
responsible sources
FSC® C018179

Penguin Random House is committed to a
sustainable future for our business, our readers
and our planet. This book is made from Forest
Stewardship Council® certified paper.

contents

introduction

'I'm afraid the parenting advice to come out of developmental psychology is very boring:
pay attention to your kids and love them.'

Professor Alison Gopnik

Well done! You have successfully loved and cared for your newborn baby and guided him or her as they have developed from a helpless infant to a walking, talking toddler. Sometimes, at the toddler stage, it can feel like all that hard work and experience counts for very little as toddlers are so different from babies.

The good news is that over your first months with your baby you bonded and got to know lots about them. You are the world expert in your baby, and with a little understanding about toddlers, their minds and their development, you will be able to carry on and feel confident as you guide and love your toddler through this unique and invigorating stage in life.

The Calm and Happy Toddler has, at its foundation, four simple 'pillars' of parenting that will stand you and your toddler in good stead:

1. warmth
2. boundaries
3. consistency
4. being present

Who am I and what do I know about toddlers?

I am a mum to three lovely children (Miranda, Benedict and Iris) and I have a PhD in Child Development and Parenting. My potted history is as follows: I was lucky enough to complete my PhD at the Sub-Department of Animal Behaviour at the University of Cambridge. This might seem a strange place to study children (or perhaps not!) but the department has a long history of exploring the bond between parent and child, whether in primates (such as the world-famous work done by Jane Goodall on chimpanzees) or as in my work, which looked at bonding and behaviour in humans. I didn't have children at that time but will never forget the powerful lessons I learned from the mums and children who came along to my laboratory to take part in the experiments I developed.

During my PhD I became a firm believer that all this wonderful research should be shared with the public, so I left Cambridge and moved to the BBC Science Department. There I worked on many programmes about understanding human behaviour. The experiments I developed were used in the television series *Child of Our Time,* presented by Professor Robert Winston. With the support of Professor Winston I co-founded The Essential Parent Company with a BBC colleague, Diana Hill, and together we launched *The Essential Baby Care Guide* (the world's first visual parenting guide). The guide is narrated by Professor Winston, with onscreen experts from The Royal College of Paediatrics, Child Health and UNICEF, among others.

The Essential Baby Care Guide provides demos to new parents on those things that are hard to read in a book, for example, how to latch on a baby to breastfeed, how to do the glass test to identify a meningitis rash, and what your baby's poo should look like! The guide is now used by parents, NHS maternity hospitals, health visitors, GPs, the NCT and even by The Royal College of Paediatrics to help train junior doctors. I continue to spend a lot of time researching and assessing the best evidence-based information for new parents.

The early years in a child's life are so vital for development, happiness and resilience. This book shares what I've learned about the precious and wonderful time when your baby begins to become mobile and assert his or her independence in the world. Toddlerhood and toddlers are wonderful and I hope my book brings you and your toddler calmness, understanding and happiness.

How to use this book

Remember: you are the world expert in your own toddler! As a parent who has already successfully looked after your baby for well over a year you should feel confident that no one loves and understands your toddler like you do. A one-size-fits-all approach can't work for everyone; I want this book to encourage and hone *your* own expertise.

This book aims to provide you with ideas that take into account your toddler's developmental stage, personality, temperament and physiology. By understanding how your toddler thinks and what changes she is going through, you can respond with confidence and stop sweating the small stuff.

Whether you need help with tantrums, night-waking, potty training or fussy eating you'll find:

- tactics to help you cope with every toddler scenario
- research from child psychologists to help you understand why your toddler is behaving like that in that moment
- toddler milestones for each area of development to show you how your toddler is changing, and how best to enjoy and encourage her mental, social and emotional development
- ideas to help you through the common toddler hurdles that all parents go through, from potty learning to tantrums and everything in between.

You can either go straight to an area that you are 'fire fighting' with your toddler or you can read a whole section on, for example, cognitive development to help put your toddler's behaviour into an overall context. Or you can map where your toddler is on the 'quick look milestone charts' in each development section (physical development, language and social development, emotional development and cognitive development) (see pages 36, 50, 65 and 88) to help you gauge the help and support your toddler needs now.

I have included some suggestions for mini 'quizzes' you can do with your toddler to get a better understanding of how her mind is working, what she understands, and how she is changing over time.

The quizzes are not scientifically rigorous and they are not meant to pigeonhole you or your toddler; they simply give you a framework to help you explore your toddler's behaviour, development and personality in order to gain understanding and confidence as a parent.

Some of them have been adapted from questionnaires developed to help psychologists assess aspects of parenting, child behaviour and development, but they are my attempt at helping you think and gauge your toddler's behaviour in a structured way...without feeling stressed or judged or like a failure. They should allow you to switch off your internal parenting critic and instead understand your toddler now and calmly think about a solution to a particular challenge you are experiencing with your toddler.

It's important that you don't allow your results to these quizzes to act as a substitute for a one-to-one consultation with a healthcare professional or educational expert. These quizzes are not designed to diagnose but rather to stimulate reflection and help you to digest some of the information in the chapter. Always speak to your doctor or health visitor if you are concerned about your toddler and do not be falsely reassured by me or friends trying to 'say the right thing.'

In Part 2 we look at classic toddler challenges and the chapters often end with a quiz or little test to try out with your toddler and a top tip. Take away 'top tips' were always something I strived to include when I worked on documentaries at the BBC. There is so much information to absorb and as a busy parent it can help to have a 'take home' message or top tip to try out.

> Throughout the book I refer to the toddler as 'she' or 'her' or 'he' or 'him'. This is for ease of reading and gender-balance, but doesn't assume that toddler boys are identical to toddler girls.

Welcome to toddlerhood

The relationship between parent and child is ever-evolving. Toddlerhood is a huge stage for parents and their toddlers to get to grips with, and it can really feel like everything you have learned as parent to your baby is not working any more. During the transition to toddler from baby your child will become more mobile, will start to communicate and talk, may develop a will of iron, and she has a *lot* of new things to learn.

Toddlerhood is a metamorphosis, and as a parent of a toddler you need to adapt and change your strategies to support and enjoy your toddler. You will need to feel your way and develop confidence as you get used to your unique toddler. This book doesn't seek to prescribe a list of techniques to 'control' your toddler. Rather, I suggest a more holistic approach. This begins by guiding you through a process of understanding your toddler and how best to enjoy this amazing phase. That isn't to say *anything* goes. There are some things that every toddler needs, and every parent needs to provide. They are:

- love and warmth
- boundaries and limits

- consistency
- being present
- secure and sensitive base.

Your toddler's brain is amazing

By the time your toddler is two, her brain will have tripled in weight since birth; the first two years of your child's life are a critical period for her development. This can sometimes feel like a lot of pressure for a parent – to be the custodian of such a precious and miraculous brain. The good news is that toddlers don't need complicated schedules and specialist education; the most important thing your child needs is your love.

A loving parent can provide all that you need to meet your child's emotional, physical and cognitive needs. A loving parent:

- spends a lot of time talking and listening to their toddler (even if their toddler is not talking yet)
- cuddles their toddler a lot, and provides a secure base for him or her to explore life
- provides calm boundaries and routines so that toddlers feel secure during their day-to-day life
- understands and treats their toddler as a unique individual
- respects his or her feelings (even if the emotions may seem extreme!).

Your toddler is a student and a teacher

Toddlers are very good at knowing intuitively what they need to learn. They are drawn to the new and are good at integrating physical play with what they need to learn in life. Toddlers have an instinct for language and a natural curiosity to engage with living things. They are industrious, open-minded and full of wonder. Seeing the world through a toddler's eyes reminds us of how wonderful and truly awesome it is.

As you come to get to know your toddler and understand her motives and understanding of the world, you will quickly become the world expert in your toddler. By not thinking that one expert can dole out one list of commandments that works for all toddlers, all parents and all situations, I hope you will feel empowered and confident enough to enjoy the fantastic ride that is toddlerhood.

Good luck!

part one

toddler development

We begin with an overview of toddler personalities and what factors can shape this. Gender, birth order, temperament and even your parenting style can all have an interesting effect.

We will also look at what happens to your child during toddlerhood in terms of physical, social, emotional and cognitive development. This is also when language develops. Your toddler is going to be very busy!

chapter one

every toddler is unique

'Always be yourself, express yourself, have faith in yourself, do not go out and look for a successful personality and duplicate it.'

Bruce Lee

Just look around any playground and you can see that toddlers come in all shapes and sizes; no two children are the same. You will see boys and girls. Some are shy, some are bold, some like to sit quietly and others want to be at the top of the climbing frame.

Every toddler is raised in a different environment. Even siblings raised by the same parents in the same home have a different environment as there is now a sibling present! Middle-borns, first-borns, an only child, a child with lots of cousins ... they will all experience the world in their own way. Having a brother or a sister, or both, will also influence your child's personality.

There are toddlers with old parents, young parents, extended families, gay parents, heterosexual parents. The personality and life-experience of the parents will have an impact, whether they are firm or permissive, happy-go-lucky or strict. You can imagine how complicated it gets when you start to mix up all these potential influences on a toddler, for example a bold, girl toddler with four older brothers being brought up with a Grandma living in the home and an older mum and a younger dad compared to a shy boy who is the only child to teenage parents.

Toddlers come as this amazing and unique 'compote' of genes, environment and epigenetic effects (where the environment actually affects how genes are expressed and whether they are switched on or not, see page 60).

You need to trust yourself as a parent and an observer – you are your toddler's equivalent of Jane Goodall and Diane Fossey, in that you have spent hours, days, months, nights and days getting to know everything about your toddler. You have got up-close and watched and noticed your toddler from all angles.

In order to give you confidence and put your observations into context I have outlined some of the types that toddle the earth:

Gender

I have raised two toddler girls and one toddler boy – which is too small a sample size to make *any* sensible conclusions about the differences or similarities between boys and girls from my personal experience. I also think that toddler brains and development actually overshadow any differences between the sexes at this age. Everything I have written in this book is applicable to toddler boys and toddler girls. However, if you look at large populations of toddlers, studies have reported that there are some different trends between toddler boys and toddler girls: Girl toddlers are more likely to:

- attend to people's faces and emotions (but, guess what, my son is more empathetic than my daughters)
- talk earlier. But gender only represents 3 per cent of the variance in toddlers' verbal skills. Research has shown that environmental exposure to language opportunity is more important than gender (my girls did talk earlier)
- potty train earlier (hardly any difference between my toddlers).

Boy toddlers are more likely to be:

- better at spatial skills that rotate 3D objects (but, guess what, my sister is a mathematician, my elder daughter is great at maths and a Minecraft fiend building virtual theme parks and towns)
- more represented in the most active subset of toddlers (not much difference in my toddlers)
- more aggressive. It is hard to know if aggression in girls is stamped out more from a young age. (Not much difference in my toddlers, but my youngest girl is the greatest lover of wrestling.)

My message here is that the toddler years are not a time to get hung up on statistical differences between boy toddlers and girl toddlers. Don't let these trends influence your expectations of boys or girls and try not to contribute to stereotypical beliefs about girls and boys. You might be interested to know that while there are no significant gender differences in age at walking, parents statistically and consistently overestimate their boy's walking skills and consistently underestimate their girl's walking skills. Try not to limit your toddler in this way.

I think there is a huge and increasing problem in gender-stereotyping children, and it is driven by marketing and consumerism. When I was a child in the 1970s and 1980s, there were more limited clothing options and toys like Lego were marketed to children as a whole. Fast-forward to today and when you walk into a children's clothes shop or toy department it's like an apartheid. If you want to choose non-pink clothes for your daughter you will need to go into the 'boys' section. Even more insidious, in my opinion, is the way that toys about science and building are often put in the branded boys' section and the toys about art and creativity are put in the branded girls' section. Driven by a desire to maximise profits, retail can limit children and reduces their freedom to explore the world. Don't be afraid to dress your daughter in dinosaur T-shirts or let your son play with cooking toys.

> When preschool children used to visit my laboratory to take part in some experiments I would let them choose a toy as a thank-you at the end of the visit. Interestingly, girls were generally allowed by their parent to choose any present they wanted, but if boys picked up a doll they were always (literally *always*) told to put it back and choose something else.

Birth order

There are a lot of stereotypes about birth order and I am wary that these can be limiting to an individual. Studies of children and adults have found some consistent differences between first-born children, middle children and last-born children that can be helpful to us when trying to understand toddlers.

First-born children are thought to relate primarily to adults and seek their approval above all. For this reason, first-born children are more likely to be obedient and conservative in their choices. Last-born children need to find their role in the family as they develop and get older. They try to find a niche that isn't already taken, so are more likely to take a different path or be rebellious.

Parents are found to be more relaxed with later-born children; you might have experienced the same inconsistency in your own family. An eldest child can have the most restrictions on their behaviour, and parents can become more permissive with each subsequent child. It's as if parents 'practise' on their first-born and calibrate their parenting as they have subsequent children.

One example with my own parenting was introducing solid foods. I was very nervous about starting solids with my first baby and read and bought lots of books. By the time my third baby started solids I was so laid back that I no longer produced Masterchef-quality purées, one vegetable at a time, and 'baby-led weaning' came naturally.

Another big difference between my first-born and my middle and last-born was the lack of scheduled events in the lives of the latter toddlers. Whereas my first toddler went to endless swimming, craft and yoga classes, the other two spent their mornings accompanying their big sister to nursery and then school. At first I felt guilty about this, but over time I've felt that my younger two actually enjoyed lots of benefits learned by 'going with the flow'.

All these differences will play out with your toddler, and I am sure you will recognise these patterns in your own family.

Toddler personalities

Toddlers come in all sizes and shapes and their temperaments are similarly wildly varied. Developmental psychologists have reported persistent differences in the temperament of babies as young as three months old. These personality or temperamental differences appear fairly hard-wired and tend to persist through childhood. So your baby has her own distinct temperament right from the start! It's important that you learn to respect and understand your baby's unique personality.

Extroverts and introverts

If you go to a birthday party or playgroup is your toddler the loud one racing about or is your toddler on the periphery watching? Anyone can see that there are some toddlers who are introverted and shy, and others who are very outgoing.

Extroverts tend to be energised by being in a group and introverts tend to find large groups of people tiring and over-whelming. Extroverts like people, groups and noise; it's like a fuel and an inspiration to them. Conversely, introverts may be social and friendly but they feel drained by large groups of people. Their fuel, creativity and drive comes from within.

There is no right or wrong way to be and both introverts and extroverts can be happy, successful and enjoy good friendships. In Western countries extroversion is often more highly rated than introversion, and parents sometimes feel they need to encourage their toddler to be more outgoing. It is important to encourage your child to be confident and speak up in social situations but it's important to remember that some of the biggest thinkers and contributors to Western society have been introverts – Albert Einstein, Rosa Parks and Bill Gates to name just three. In personality tests 30–50 per cent of people are rated as introverts. Introverts are also not necessarily shy; they may just be self-contained and content.

Risk-takers

Is your toddler physically timid or bold? The one at the top of the climbing frame or the one preferring to have you close as she climbs? Temperamental differences are ancient in the animal kingdom (my husband, an evolutionary biologist, has even found bold and timid temperaments amongst individual fish in a shoal).

Brain imaging studies have found that bold, fearless children appear to have a less sensitive amygdala (this is an ancient part of the brain that makes us take action when we are in danger). These bold children are pretty unflappable, happy to approach strangers and tend to be risk-takers. This can be pretty nerve-wracking as a parent as it may feel as if your toddler has no 'common sense'. In contrast, risk-avoiding children appear to have a more sensitive amygdala. These children may feel overwhelmed by a stimulus, e.g. a firework that hardly even registers in a bold child's brain.

There are 'costs and benefits' to these temperamental differences, which is why you find a variety within populations. In evolutionary terms, sometimes being bold pays off: if you dare to forage whilst predators are around, you will take in more calories than those that don't brave it out. However, taking that risk might be a deadly decision and the more timid individuals live to forage another day. So try not to see these differences as good or bad – they are just a natural variety.

If you have a bold, fearless toddler you will need to encourage her to stop and think and be safe. If you have a timid and fearful toddler you will need to encourage her to take a few risks, enjoy new physical feats, and get used to some uncertainty.

Boisterous toddlers

You don't need me to tell you that it is completely normal for toddlers to be full of energy and loud and boisterous. However, even amongst the toddler tribe some members seem to be even louder and even more boisterous than their peers. The parent of the boisterous toddler is the one who never gets to sit down and sneak a restorative cup of tea at the playgroup. Although their energy can be infectious, there are times when it can be exhausting being their mum or dad.

It is wonderful to see the energy and enthusiasm that a boisterous toddler exhibits. Your 'Tigger' will need even more outside play than other toddlers. Central to this play should be lots of opportunities to take safe risks such as climbing on the climbing frame. So many of us live very sedentary lives and we tend to underestimate how much exercise and fresh air our children need. You need to be disciplined about giving your toddler lots of fresh air in much the same way as a dog owner that has a breed that needs a lot of walking does!

Parents have told me that it can be hard work dealing with other adults, who are perhaps not used to being near lively toddlers. If a disapproving adult is a grandparent or elderly neighbour that can make it very hard for you. However, we are not living in the Victorian era, where self-centred adults truly believed that children should be seen but not heard. As a society that happily keeps toddlers in little ghettos away from the serious worker adults, I think we all need to be a bit more realistic about the needs of toddlers who are part of our society. We have pretty deluded ideas about how much being quiet and sitting still toddlers can achieve. I am sure some adults think that public space is *adult* space, and babies, toddlers, teenagers and even the elderly are not really welcome. Try not to take it personally; you can't respect someone's opinion if they truly believe that a toddler should act just like an adult. Toddlers are not adults and even the most disapproving adult was a toddler once!

Although adults need a bit of a reality check about toddlers, for the most part all children need to begin to learn there are times when they need to talk more quietly, walk, and be a bit careful. You can make your toddler aware that she needs to be careful around, for example, an elderly person who might be very nervous of falling, or a young baby.

TOP TIP

Make sure your toddler has had a really good run around outside and lunch before you meet up with a disapproving relative or start a long car journey. Your toddler will be at their most calm and more likely to cope with the next part of her day.

Toddlers need us to help them regulate their emotions and parents have the ability to do something quite amazing – when you talk calmly and slowly, and slow down your breathing, your toddler will subconsciously copy you. This is called 'matching' behaviour and is amazingly powerful. See if you can notice when you are talking to someone – you also tend to match and copy patterns of breathing, posture and movement.

Conversely, if you scream, cajole and hyperventilate you will wind both of you up. So remember to channel Derren Brown the next time you want to bring back your boisterous toddler from out of orbit!

Cautious toddlers

Whilst it is normal for toddlers to be full of energy, some toddlers will be much more quiet, anxious and nervous than their peers. It appears that this 'behavioural inhibition' may be down, in part, to having a sensitive amygdala that fires a warning at a lower threshold than in other bolder individuals. Harvard University psychologist Jerome Kagan termed this 'behavioural inhibition' and reported stable temperamental difference in babies as young as three months old. He ran studies where children would come to his laboratory every few years to play games and complete tasks. To assess behavioural inhibition he had stimuli such as a robot with bright flashing lights and whirring noises. Whereas the bold children ran to investigate the toy, the more behaviourally inhibited children displayed fear and avoidance of the robot.

If you have a cautious toddler you will need to be respectful and patient with her. Don't force her to do things that scare her; instead approach new situations with baby steps. If she hates the music group of toddlers banging drums, respect the fact that she finds the noise overwhelming (don't we all!).

I gave the children in my doctoral study fearful (see page 170) tasks to complete. It consisted of a big black box with a hole in the top. The parent was asked to see if their child would like to reach in and remove the 'scary' objects from it (they were rubber creepy crawlies).

The parents who were the most sensitive and successful with their children on this task were the ones who felt no 'performance anxiety' towards me as a researcher and instead remained child-centred (by this I mean their focus was on the child's experience and feelings, not their own agenda). The parents offered to do the task first and reassured their child when it was her turn. I learned a lot from the 'low-anxiety' mothers about how to lead from the front. The key is not worrying about being 'seen to parent'. Parenting is not meant to be a spectator sport, but we are social creatures and we tend to worry about how other people appraise our toddlers and how we appear as parents. It can help you and your toddler if you try to switch off this internal critic. It's hard enough to look after a toddler without having the extra layer of social stress to 'be the perfect parent with the perfect child'. This kind of 'performance anxiety' can sabotage your ability to parent your toddler effectively; instead focus on your connection with her and what she is experiencing and feeling.

How parenting style affects toddler behaviour

> 'All happy families resemble one another, but each unhappy family is unhappy in its own way.'
>
> *Anna Karenina*, Leo Tolstoy

I think Tolstoy hit the nail on the head with this statement that opens his novel *Anna Karenina*. Happy families all share the same trait: they love and respect each other. These are the main things that your toddler will need to thrive. That said, parents are as unique as their toddlers, and we all come to parenting with our own histories, philosophies and hopes. This can feel like a huge responsibility as a parent, but the good news is that some simple and effective changes in your parenting style can really promote happy and positive development in your toddler.

Attachment theory

The bond between you and your toddler is perhaps the most profound way that your parenting style affects her 'personality'. John Bowlby developed his Attachment Theory after his observations of children needing long-term care in hospitals.

The belief of the time, back in the 1930s, was that parents should drop off children at hospital and only see them when they were discharged. The flawed thinking was that it spared the child from the sadness of saying goodbye each day. Bowlby challenged this belief and today parents frequently stay overnight on paediatric wards.

Attachment Theory believes that as human babies are so helpless at birth, they need to bond with caregivers who are warm, consistent and loving. These caregivers (usually parents, though in Bowlby's case, it was his beloved nanny) provide their children with a secure base from which to explore the world. In the toddler years this idea of a secure base comes to the fore as toddlers want to explore and learn about the outside world but need a touchstone to keep them safe and to reassure them.

Mary Ainsworth went on to assess the different attachment relationships that children had with their parents. She developed a laboratory test called the 'Strange Situation Test' which allowed her to watch how mothers and children (aged 12–18 months) said goodbye, and how they reunited during a short visit to the lab. The table (below) shows how the toddlers behaved during the project.

	Secure	Insecure–Ambivalent	Insecure–Avoidant
Separation anxiety	Distressed when mum leaves	Intensely distressed when mum leaves	No sign of distress when mum leaves
Stranger anxiety	Avoids stranger when alone but friendly when mum present	Avoids the stranger and displays fear of stranger	Toddler fine with the stranger and keeps playing
Reunion	Full eye contact with mum. Positive & happy when mum returns	Approaches mother but ambivalent; resists contact; may show anger	Shows little interest when mum returns
% of infants	70	15	15

Secure attachment to a parent is the foundation of happy toddlers and good mental health. Toddlers are more likely to be securely attached to their parents if their parents are warm, consistent and sensitive to their needs.

The concept of attachment has been taken on board by the 'attachment parenting' movement in the West. Attachment parenting has a child-centred philosophy and looks to traditional parenting practices, such as extended breastfeeding, baby-wearing and co-sleeping. This is a traditional parenting style in many parts of the world.

'Good-enough' parenting

Donald Winnicott was a paediatrician and psychologist and a peer of John Bowlby. He published his concept of the 'good-enough parent' in 1949. This flouted the idea that parents are supposed to be perfect and endlessly patient beings that prevent their children from encountering any conflict or strife in life. Winnicott claimed that mothers were real people with real emotions, and this actually facilitated their children's development. I think this idea is reassuring to all parents: that you don't have to be perfect, that although flawed, if you try your best for your toddler, and are loving and consistent, she will thrive.

real parent story

Lucy (Daniel, 3 years and Amy, 1 year)

'I thought I knew what toddlers were like after I had Daniel but Amy was just such a different baby and toddler. Daniel slept really well and ate anything and was very placid. Amy was hard to settle at night and a really picky eater – her whole personality was completely different, she was a little firecracker and still is!'

Quiz: Is your toddler extrovert or introvert?

1. On a quiet afternoon at home, how does your toddler respond?
   a) She gets very fed up quickly and pesters me for attention.
   b) She will play for a while but then starts to bounce off the walls.
   c) She is very happy to play by herself in her room and is often utterly engrossed in an activity.

2. When you give your toddler her favourite book, how does she respond?
   a) She loves me to read the book with her and shares lots of eye contact throughout.
   b) She loves to share the book with me but sometimes flicks through the book by herself.
   b) She does like me to read her a story but often gets completely absorbed in the book herself and looks at the pictures and turns the pages herself.

3. Does your toddler interrupt what you are doing?
   a) She is forever calling my attention, showing me what she's doing, starting a conversation with me and anyone else around.
   b) If she's bored she will interrupt me a lot, but if she's occupied she doesn't try and get my attention.
   c) She rarely interrupts me or tries to get my attention unless she's really keen to show me something she's interested in.

4. Does your toddler like to join in with games and silliness?
   a) She's always in the thick of it and gets stuck in with energy to games with others.
   b) If she knows everyone involved she will often take part in games but isn't particularly vocal.
   c) She tends to watch from the sidelines but will join in if she knows people well and is interested in the game.

5. How does your toddler respond to crowded, busy places?
   a) The louder and the busier the setting the more excited she gets. It makes her louder and more energised.
   b) She doesn't mind crowded or busy settings.
   c) She tends to withdraw and find crowded settings overwhelming.

6. Is your toddler a better talker or listener?
   a) Even before she could speak she would always be chatting, using noises and lots of body language. She often doesn't wait for a response.
   b) She's interested in what other people are doing and gives people time to speak.
   c) She's very observant and listens well, but is often hesitant about responding.

7. How are your toddler's energy levels after a party or event?
   a) She's happy, energetic and bouncing off the walls after a party – she is the original party animal!
   b) She's sometimes excited and sometimes tired after big events.
   c) She seems really exhausted after big parties, especially if she's had to take part in group activities.

8. Does your toddler have a party piece?
   a) She loves to be the centre of attention and show everyone and anyone her favourite new dance or skill.
   b) She will 'show off' her party piece if asked and if it's close family and friends.
   c) She really seems to dislike being the centre of attention and often refuses to show others something she can do.

9. If your toddler is sad or upset how can you tell?
   a) Everybody can tell, she cries loudly and lets everyone know she's not happy.
   b) She has the occasional loud meltdown, but often she is comforted by a quiet cuddle.
   c) If she's sad she can really withdraw into herself and not want to interact with anyone.

Mostly As: Your toddler seems like an extrovert already. She is energised by people and social events and can seem a bit lost in her own company. You can help her to enjoy quiet time with her favourite books or toys, but she will enjoy and crave lots of activities.

Mostly Bs: Your toddler has both extrovert and introvert tendencies. Whilst she enjoys being with other people, big groups and parties can also be tiring.

Mostly Cs: Your toddler seems to be an introvert. She loves to have time for her own games and imagination. She finds big groups and parties tiring, even if she enjoys them. She will flourish with time to herself but will benefit from being encouraged to enjoy sharing activities with small groups of friends.

TOP TIP

Don't worry about saying 'no' to your toddler. Parents can get very worried about setting boundaries for toddlers as they've never had to do it before. If you can lay fair and consistent boundaries your time as a parent will be easier.

chapter two

physical development

'Don't run before you can walk.'

English idiom

Seeing your baby metamorphose into an active toddler is such an exciting part of being a parent. Toddlers hit the classic developmental milestones at different times, though generally in the same order of development. The old saying 'don't run before you can walk' recognises this point and each stage of development builds on what went before.

One of the main drivers of your toddler's cognitive, emotional and even language development is their underlying physical development. Being able to move around the environment to investigate new places, new toys and new people means your toddler has new perspectives that lead to fresh thoughts and concepts.

If you feel your toddler is behind his peers it can be stressful. There are big variations between toddlers and developmental milestones are a rather crude way of measuring progress. Think of them as guidelines and not a strict timeline; they can help parents and healthcare professionals to spot when a child might be exhibiting developmental delay and need a little extra help and support.

Coordinated movement

We are symmetrical animals, with an invisible 'line of symmetry' running from the top of our head down to our toes, passing between the eyes and nipples. Our brains have two hemispheres and the way they control our symmetrical body is very interesting in relation to toddler development and coordination. The right side of the brain controls movement in the left side of the body, and the left side of the brain controls movement in the right side of the body. Between both hemispheres of the brain is a structure called the corpus callosum that connects all communication between each side.

When your child passes a toy from his left hand to his right hand this is one example of 'crossing the midline' (down the centre of the body) and it is an important neurological development. Another example of crossing the midline is when the right hand can cross over the midline and touch or pick up an object on their left-hand side, and vice versa. Crossing the midline requires 'bilateral integration' with neural activity between both the left and right cerebral hemispheres. This integration of the whole symmetrical body allows the two sides of the body to move together in coordination with one another. It is a vital part of locomotion, such as crawling and walking, as the movements require harmonious turn-taking of each side of the body. Crawling, with opposite arms and legs crossing the diagonal, is the first coordinated action that requires crossing the midline.

THE CLOCK SONG

At the 'Birthlight' baby and toddler yoga group that I took my eldest toddler to, we did a lovely exercise with Sally Lomas that encouraged crossing the midline called The Clock Song. You can try this at home. With your toddler lying on his back, take his right hand and bring it to his left foot, holding his ankle and wrist. Bring his hand and foot together gently at each tick, and move them back with each tock. The song goes:

The Grandfather clock goes tick tock, tick tock, tick tock,
The clock on the wall goes tick tock, tick tock, tick tock,
And all the little watches go tickticktickticktickticktickTOCK!

The speed gets faster with each new clock. Swap to take his left hand to touch his right foot. The idea is that each time the limbs touch and cross the midline, your toddler's brain improves his sense of symmetry and coordination.

It's a lovely game and all my children loved it, especially as it sped up. I've never seen a paper reporting that the clock game improved crossing the midline integration, but done gently I doubt it does any harm and it might just help. Whatever the case, it's certainly fun!

Crawling and walking

Crawling begins from around seven months but not all babies will crawl – lots of babies bum-shuffle or just begin moving by pulling themselves up to cruise walk.

Walking is the developmental breakthrough that defines the term 'toddler'; when your baby learns to walk … or toddle … she is by definition a toddler! Children walk on average at around 13 months old, but there is a wide range, with most (98 per cent) walking by 18 months. Help him practise walking by holding hands; this stimulates development of the part of the brain which controls his balance and coordination.

If your toddler has got to 18 months of age without learning to walk alone, the chances are that all will be fine, but 18 months is the perfect time to get him checked. Ask your GP to refer him to your local child development team and they will do a full check.

Climbing stairs

If your toddler started walking around his first birthday you will probably find that by around 16 months old, your toddler will be able to hold your hand and walk up and down stairs.

Walking upstairs is a bit easier and safer than going down again, and for a while he will have to do one step at a time. By the time your toddler is three years old he may be able to walk up using alternate feet, though I remember my own toddlers favoured taking one step at a time beyond that age as they were short for their age. It would have been interesting to see what they would have done on tiny steps, but toddlers generally have to contend with a world built for adults – it drives me mad when hand driers, sinks and handwash are all out of reach for our child population!

Going downstairs involves all the muscles contracting in a completely opposite pattern from going upstairs. It's much harder as it requires more core strength, which toddlers don't have much of yet (hence their delightful little egg-shaped bellies). Toddlers tend to sink onto their bottoms, sensibly, and shuffle down one step at a time. Toddlers will need to be supervised on the stairs until they master them safely.

Running and jumping

By the time your toddler is around two years old he will probably be able to run. He still might be a little unsteady on his feet and have to run in one direction, but it is a gait that toddlers embrace with huge enthusiasm.

Jumping is trickier than running and comes much later. In order to jump, your toddler needs to be able to push off or up with both legs simultaneously. At first there will be many unsynchronised attempts at jumping with one leg followed by the other leg. This leads to very short, sideways jumps.

A great place to practise jumping is to put on your wellies and go jumping up and down in muddy puddles. By the time your toddler is approaching his third birthday he should be able to do what PE teachers used to refer to as a 'standing broad jump' where he jumps forward on two legs. Trampets with handles, trampolines and beds with guards are all fun ways to practise jumping as your toddler gets older.

Hopping and kicking

It takes a lot of coordination, core strength and balance to be able to keep one foot off the floor to be able to hop, skip or kick a ball. You will be able to enjoy kicking a football with your toddler around his second birthday. Hopping comes quite a bit later as only two-fifths of three-year-old children can stand on one leg. By the time they are five the vast majority of children can hop.

Toddler yoga

Toddlers are absolute naturals at yoga and classes are fairly easy to find now. Yoga classes offer safe, careful exercises for your toddler's developing body and are designed to promote strength, coordination and balance both in still poses and with movement.

Each movement and pose is explained in a toddler-friendly way, using phrases like:

- child pose

- cat pose

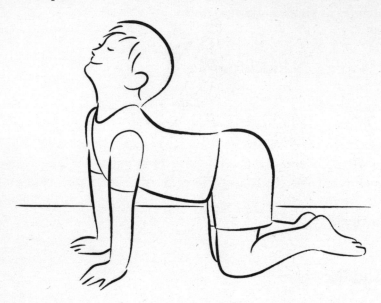

- dog pose

- tree pose

- lion roar

- bow pose

You may already be familiar with these names and poses from adult yoga classes.

You might also work together; for example, in the Superman pose your toddler will balance like Superman on your feet as you lie on your back and hold him steady with your hands.

Self-care skills

Feeding himself, going to the toilet, washing hands, getting dressed and other self-care skills are all very useful for your toddler and instil confidence when achieved.

Feeding

Your toddler starts by self-feeding with finger food, and by 18 months he may be trying to use a spoon and fork. He will initially use a fork to stab food rather than hold it still while he cuts with a knife. Using utensils as adults do probably won't occur until your child turns four. Eating together at a table really helps to develop these fine motor skills and basic table manners.

Hand-washing

You can get your toddler in the habit of regular hand-washing before mealtimes, especially if he is eating finger food. Hand-washing is also an essential part of potty learning. I recommend a step-up block (ideally at a low sink) so that he can practise using the tap, wetting hands, soaping and rinsing. This can take ages, and most toddlers will need a bit of help drying their hands, but in my experience toddlers tend to enjoy the hand-washing ritual.

Teeth cleaning and bathing

Your toddler may want to clean his own teeth from around 18 months old, however, dentists recommend that you will need to help your child clean his teeth until at least eight years old to make sure he does it properly. It is important to encourage his attempts to clean his teeth.

Although you will need to help him wash his hair and face, my toddlers always started by washing their own tummies and knees in the bath with a soapy flannel.

Dressing and undressing

Taking off clothes is easier than putting clothes on. Toddlers all seem to enjoy undressing, streaking and being naked, and taking off clothes is an important life skill that most toddlers begin between their first and second birthday. Getting dressed requires much more dexterity and planning. Your toddler won't be able to balance standing up while he puts his feet into trousers and pull them up until he is about four. Your toddler will find a loose T-shirt the easiest item of clothing at first, as he can sit down to put it on, and the arm holes are short and easy to wriggle his arms through. Expect heads to try to come through arm holes more often than not! He will also be able to put on slip-on shoes if they aren't too tight. My daughter at 6 has been known to put shoes on the wrong feet so double-check before you leave home!

MILESTONES OF PHYSICAL DEVELOPMENT

Here is an overview of the order and timing of major milestones in physical development. Remember, there is always a normal range around these average timings with half reaching the milestone earlier than average and half meeting the milestone later than average.

By 13 months

- 50 per cent of toddlers can walk in one direction, with frequent falls.

By 15 months

- generally able to walk alone
- can post small items into a hole
- can point at preferred items
- ambidextrous (can use either hand) but starting to show a preference for using one hand
- throws and drops toys on purpose and enjoy the cause and effect
- uses whole hand to grip a crayon.

By 18 months

- 98 per cent of toddlers can walk
- can kneel and squat
- can run in one direction
- can begin to thread large beads onto thick string
- shakes items out of receptacle container
- builds towers of three or more bricks.

By 24 months

- can run and able to slalom to avoid obstacles
- climbs onto furniture

- can throw but not catch
- climbs stairs one at a time
- enjoys a scooter or balance bike
- jumps off a step
- draws circles, vertical lines and dots
- able to scoop up food with a spoon.

By 30 months

- has a preferred hand to hold a crayon
- builds towers of over seven blocks with his preferred hand.

By 36 months

- able to walk sideways and backwards
- can pedal a tricycle
- can kick and catch a big soft ball if hands are outstretched
- uses preferred hand to build a tower over nine blocks high
- uses thumb and two fingers to hold a crayon (known as the 'dynamic tripod grasp') and starts to use child scissors
- can draw the letter 'H'
- draws people with limbs coming out of head
- can stab soft food with a fork and scoop with a spoon.

Physical development problems

If your toddler favours one arm or one leg when he moves, such as crawling in a lop-sided way, this might indicate better strength or coordination on one side. A preference for one hand over the other doesn't tend to emerge until 18 months, so preference at 12 months may be a sign of a problem with the left side of his body. If you notice any asymmetry in your toddler's physical development it will never do any harm to get it checked out by your GP; your toddler can be assessed by your local child development team if there are any concerns.

DID YOU KNOW?

A study of A&E diagnosis reported that the best predictor of how ill a child was, was the parents' level of anxiety about the illness. A doctor on shift at A&E has no idea of what your toddler is usually like and it is your responsibility to act as an advocate for your child and help the doctor to put your child's symptoms firmly in the context of what is normal for your child. Remember that no one else knows your toddler like you do; from how often they poo to if they've had an allergic reaction ... or they are just 'not themselves'. You are the most accurate barometer to your child's health and development.

HOW IS YOUR TODDLER GETTING ON?

There is so much that can be achieved to help and support toddlers who have developmental delay that it is really worth getting an early diagnosis and support if needed. However, as with all aspects of parenting, it can be a fine line to tread between getting overly anxious about non-existent problems. Always remember though that you are the expert in your child. Here are some pointers to help guide you.

First birthday check

By the time your toddler has turned one he should be able to eat finger food and climb onto and off a small step.

18 month check

By the time your toddler turns 18 months old, your toddler should be able to walk, take off his shoes and be able to mark paper with a crayon. His walking gait should be heel-to-toe so look out for departures from this once your toddler is walking.

Second birthday check

By the time your toddler has turned two, check he can kick a ball, run, use a spoon and draw a vertical line on paper.

Third birthday check

By the time your toddler has turned three, check he can balance on one leg, throw a ball overarm, walk downstairs with alternating feet and can cut with child scissors.

Everything is a learning opportunity

As your toddler becomes increasingly mobile and dexterous, the world opens up to him. Everything is a new learning opportunity that gives rise to further development, and in turn, more questions, and a need for more language and communication skills. Here are some fun projects you can do together; they will be fun and challenging to your child and interesting for you to observe how he is getting on.

THE BLOCK TEST

Healthcare professionals often assess motor skill development in toddlers by seeing how many blocks a toddler can stack up. A set of small wood blocks (about 3 cm cubed) is a classic toy that your child will enjoy playing with, and you can observe how his motor skills are developing while he plays.

Encourage your toddler to make a tower of blocks. Give him lots of praise and encouragement and over time notice how many blocks he can stack up. As a guideline:

15 months old – 2 block stack

18 months old – 3 block stack

24 months old – 6 block stack

30 months old – can begin to stacks blocks with one hand

36 months old – may try up to a 10 block stack

real parent story

Sarah (Tom, 24 months)

'Tom didn't walk until he was 18 months old – just bum-shuffled. He was really big, on the 99th centile for weight and height and he had a big head. His head control and everything seemed a bit slower, as if his size made it harder for him to move around. All my friends' toddlers were walking from 11 months so it really stressed me out but it made his first steps all the more wonderful!'

TOP TIP

One of the best ways to encourage your toddler's physical development is to take him to the local swimming pool. Supported by you in the water (so he won't need armbands in these lessons as you hold him safely), your toddler will be free to move his whole body while being weightless. Look out for toddler water sessions; as well as being sociable, they are useful if you are unsure how to encourage water confidence.

chapter three

language and social development

'Language is the blood of the soul into which thoughts run and out of which they grow.'

Oliver Wendell Holmes

B abies and toddlers are social creatures and communication is instinctive to them. Although not able to speak at birth, babies do try to communicate, as any parent with a young baby will know! Crying is an early non-verbal form of communication. It is very powerful, and a mother hearing her baby cry will feel an overwhelming instinct to go to her baby and attend to her needs. The infant crying and the parents' response are basic survival instincts, but over time your baby's communications will become more nuanced, responsive and not just based on asking for help!

Babies and toddlers are great observers and listeners. From birth their favourite sound is that of their parents' voices and they love to look at their parents' faces. This fixation on the parent is also a crucial instinct that allows babies to learn to communicate and eventually use spoken language.

Your baby will start the long and miraculous process of learning language and communication from when they first hear and attend to your voice whilst in the womb. Tests show that babies respond to their mother's voice from around 20 weeks' gestation. This means that from even when in the uterus, she was familiar with your voice.

It is easy to take our language instinct for granted, but without it we would not be able to communicate with our loved ones, function in society, build relationships and social groups or learn. Even thinking requires language as you will use your learned language, in part, to allow you to think about people, the physical world and even our internal emotional worlds. Language allows us to stand on the shoulders of giants and quickly comprehend millennia of thoughts, ideas and breakthroughs in science and philosophy.

Encouraging language and communication skills

The best thing you can do to help your toddler to learn to communicate is to communicate with her – a lot! This can start right from birth and it really doesn't always have to be words – smiles, raspberry noises, lullabies, music, funny voices – whatever you feel like. It's all part of your toddler feeling she has your attention and that's what she loves.

This give-and-take communication is so important. Research currently under way by Professor Jonathan Green at the University of Manchester is attempting to see if teaching this give-and-take communication to the parents of quiet, non-verbal babies may help language and communication development in autistic children.

TOP TIP

When you talk to your toddler, remember to give her a chance to respond. She won't be responding with fluent language, but if you give her time you will see that she understands taking turns and has a go at responding to you from an early age with smiles, gurgles and maybe handclapping. You can even observe this from birth.

Parents tend to worry a lot about their toddler's language, partly as it seems so fundamental to their personality and ability to relate to other people. However, parents tend to worry far too much about vocabulary and pronunciation, which are by no means the fundamental building blocks of communication and language development. The key is non-verbal communication and 'passive' listening skills. Non-verbal communication skills include:

- maintaining eye contact
- smiling
- looking to a person to share an experience, such as something funny
- learning to take turns in conversation – even before babies can speak they need to learn that people take turns in communication and you need to leave time for them to respond to you
- attending and listening to someone while they speak.

Hand and body language

Toddlers can use gestures, noises and tones before they can use verbal language. Some parents will teach their toddler to sign or gesture a few key words such as: 'more', 'milk', 'hungry'. This can really help toddlers who get a bit frustrated when we can't understand what they are trying to say. You don't need to attend classes or use a specific signing language – you can make up your own simple signs and just have fun with your baby. From as early as seven months your child will start to respond and understand simple hand and body gestures such as: 'No', 'look' etc. You can build on this over time and gestures really help your toddler communicate.

Action songs are a lovely way of learning words through physical actions. It's so much fun for your toddler to sit with you whilst you're singing an action song like 'The Wheels on the Bus'.

Action songs are particularly valuable with late talkers as they can join in and communicate without using words.

Toddlers use their whole body to learn, and movement and rhythm really facilitate language learning. Music is a universal 'language' that people love to listen to, share and sing together. Notice how your toddler's face lights up and looks at you when you play a favourite song. This is a lovely early form of communication where she is looking to share the experience with you. By singing and dancing together you are communicating and 'matching' your behaviour and responses. Matching is a universal form of communication where two individuals connect by mirroring movements, body language and sounds. It is particularly powerful for non-verbal toddlers who cannot express themselves with language yet.

Taking time to talk

Did you know that the more you talk to your baby and toddler the bigger, heavier and more interconnected her brain will grow? During a toddler's first two years her brain will develop faster than it ever will again in her life. Talking with your toddler literally helps 'build' her brain, and facilitates social, emotional and cognitive development.

> **TOP TIP**
>
> The National Literacy Trust have a website called 'Talk To Your Baby' as they recognise that talking to your child from birth is the foundation of literacy, vocabulary and even good mental health. It's well worth a look.

As your toddler learns new things, her brain will be laying down pathways and connections (called synapses) between neurons in her brain. These pathways become stronger and the learning will be consolidated. It's like building a pathway through a field of long grass; the more times you walk a certain route the wider and more pronounced the path becomes. In time the path is easy to see and use, and the route is faster and better developed. Every song you sing and game you play with your toddler helps to develop her brain.

THE THREE-TIME TRICK

I have noticed that parents instinctively say a new word to their toddler, three times in succession, in different contexts, for example:

'Look at the train on the track!'

'Would you like to push the train?'

'The train is a nice pink colour.'

This makes it easier for your toddler to hear and understand the word 'train' in a stream of words. I am convinced that this instinctive three-time trick quickly allows toddlers to notice a new word and work out how to use it.

You really don't need to overthink talking to your toddler. When we use 'motherese' (or 'baby talk') we generally speak to toddlers in an optimal and instinctive way. Sentences are simplified, words are repeated, and our tone is generally positive, more high-pitched, and engaging.

If you expand the learning by not just saying the words, but also singing lullabies and doing action songs with your toddler, the parts of your toddler's brain that deal with language will be stimulated in all these contexts.

So, the more pathways you weave into a memory or concept such as music, words and even other senses like smell (which is perhaps the most evocative sense for recalling memories) the more solid that memory will be.

Remember to include the whole family. Parents can take it in turn to read each night, and older siblings and grandparents will be great too. Oral stories from your culture and your baby's grandparents really enrich their experience of language. It's a lovely and important tradition to pass on songs and stories the way they have been passed on from adult to child for as long as people have walked the earth.

A unique creature

We are the only animals that point our fingers and have whites to our eyes. One theory for why humans have developed white eyes is that it allows *other* people to look at what we are looking at. Babies don't get this immediately, but will soon look where you look and read your emotions. It's called 'social referencing' (see page 172) and toddlers are very good at it.

By the time your toddler is 12 months old she will probably have begun to point at things. This is a major developmental milestone and is your toddler's first opportunity to get people to attend to something she sees. It's a universal and powerful way of communicating within our species. If someone points, people look to where they are pointing.

When will my toddler speak?

One of the most wonderful aspects of toddlerhood is seeing your non-verbal baby become a talking toddler. There is much more to language development and communication than vocabulary. By 18 months old, toddlers generally have around 20 words that they use. However, children can generally understand more than they can say, with about 50 words understood for every word that they can say. You would expect your toddler to be able to follow simple requests before she can speak. By the time your toddler turns four years old she may have a vocabulary of around 5,000 words.

TIP BOX

I CAN, the children's communication charity, have a brilliant website that you can go to check your child's language progress: http://www.talkingpoint.org.uk It has games to play that help your child's speech and language. You can also contact an I CAN speech and language therapist.

Reading with your toddler

Reading is a lovely way to bond with your toddler. It is much less about the story and plot and much more about having your undivided attention, sitting close to you, and hearing the sound of your voice. This will lay down a love of books and reading that will make the more formal transition to phonics and literacy much easier at school. Toddlers will carry books over to their parents to read with them; they try to encourage the activity as they feel really close and bonded when sharing a book.

Toddlers love books that make them laugh. They also love to notice cause-and-effect, the rhythm of language and joining in. We are so lucky to have the most amazing books written for toddlers that contain some or all of these elements. Ask at your local library for book recommendations and free loans. My favourites include *Each Peach Pear Plum*; *The Very Hungry Caterpillar*; *Room on the Broom* and anything by Dr Seuss ... I may be showing my age slightly but even so these books are timeless and have a wonderful combination of compelling pictures and a great rhythm.

If you or your partner finds it difficult to talk to a toddler who cannot talk fluidly yet, books help to make a reason to talk together. Your toddler will probably begin to respond with squeals of delight and in time may join in with the rhyme at the end of a verse.

All the talking and listening that you do while you share a book will help to develop your baby's social and literacy skills. Studies of child development have found that children who have the opportunity to share books with their parents and have books around the home (either from the library or bought) perform better at school. Books do seem to have a special role in a child's emotional and cognitive development, and the plain joy of childhood.

Multi-language families

If you are a multi-language family or household it is wonderful to share spoken stories, books, lullabies, rhymes and songs in all the languages you speak. This will really help your baby's language skills develop, especially if you want your child to speak and understand several languages. Some children can have struggles as they learn and compartmentalise two or more languages – although it has been estimated that the majority of the world's toddlers learn more than one language. It is a miracle that a child's brain can absorb several languages, with their grammars and rules. Parents often report that their child will go through a phase of rejecting their 'mother's' tongue in favour of consolidating the native language where they are living. If you are concerned about any difficulties or frustrations your toddler is experiencing you can talk to your health visitor. It can also help your toddler to use gestures and signs to back up spoken language.

Watching television

Toddlers seem to particularly love sharing books with their parents. One reason for this is that sharing books is one activity in which they get their parent's undivided attention. When you are both watching television it can become all too easy to check Facebook, text, fold washing, daydream and not really interact with your toddler, so it just doesn't have the same benefits for your child.

Many paediatricians and developmental psychologists do not recommend much, if any, television for young toddlers (under two years), especially not as a form of educational activity. Hanging out with you, talking, singing, eating and 'helping' you around the home will generally be much more 'educational' and more importantly enjoyable and valued by your toddler.

However, there are some lovely programmes for older toddlers (over two years). As a rule of thumb I think if your toddler is watching a television programme it is better to share it in the same way you would share a book. So sit your toddler on your knee and use the programme as something to chat about rather than leaving them for long periods of time alone.

My toddlers did watch television. I usually felt better if they did so after we had come in from an activity like swimming or going for a walk. After lunch, whilst digesting our meals together, we might watch a short, well-made programme.

Some parents and educators have a 'no-TV' rule. The American Academy of Pediatrics issued a policy statement in 2011 with a 'better-safe-than-sorry' recommendation of no television before two years. Aric Sigman wrote a book called *Remotely Controlled: How television is damaging our lives*. He proposed that watching a lot of television can have many far-reaching effects on children's development, such as attention problems.

With my own children I tend to think 'everything in moderation, especially moderation.' My children have really loved watching some imaginative cartoons, such as *Totoro* made by Studio Ghibli, and I will never forget the first films that made my children cry with empathy. My elder daughter wept during *Iron Giant* when the robot sacrifices himself to save the town. On the other hand there are many more pretty bad programmes that were a relatively empty entertainment for my children.

I think it is wise to be cautious about the amount of time you let your toddler watch television. I know as a parent, I didn't want to hear that when I was tired and plonking my tiring toddler in front of the television seemed so seductive. The truth is that your toddler doesn't *need* television, so focus on promoting the activities that you know are positive: lots of talking, physical activity, fresh air and playing.

Milestones of language development

Language is incredibly complex and takes years to master. It is amazing to see a toddler begin to follow that path of milestones to understanding and using language to communicate. These milestones tend to go in the same order but some toddlers will be earlier talkers or earlier at understanding.

Language development can be broken down into:

- receptive language – understanding what people say
- expressive language – using vocabulary, sentences and grammar to express oneself
- pragmatic language – social connection to other people through language.

The key language milestones

Here are some general guidelines of what to expect in your toddler's language and communication development:

By 12–18 months

NON-VERBAL MILESTONES

- enjoys peek-a-boo (this can be enjoyed from four months)
- understands a few simple words such as 'milk', 'hat' and 'dog'

- understands and follows a few simple instructions such as 'kiss Daddy', 'give me', 'kick ball', 'stop'
- can point to family members and familiar objects such as 'where's the cup?'

VERBAL MILESTONES

- uses around 20 simple words, such as 'cup', 'daddy' and 'dog'. You will learn to recognise the words but it might sound too garbled for strangers to understand at this stage
- shares a picture book (though again some children will do this from babyhood)
- gestures or points, often with sounds and sometimes a word to show what she wants
- imitates words and gestures of familiar people
- copies lots of things that adults say and gestures that they make
- does pretend play such as pretending a brick is a phone or a shoe is a car.

By 18–24 months

NON-VERBAL MILESTONES

- concentrates on activities for longer
- enjoys pretend play with their toys, such as feeding dolly
- listens and attends to what you say for several sentences
- understands 200–500 words (no need to count!)
- understands more complex questions or instructions such as 'where is your bed?' and 'show me your toes'.

VERBAL MILESTONES

- copies noises and words
- uses 50+ words, mainly nouns

- beginning to use short sentences with two words such as 'more milk' or 'bye Mummy'
- uses a limited number of consonant sounds, e.g. d, b, h, m, n, p
- will still miss the ends off words at this stage
- mispronounces words such as words containing 'th' or 'f'
- can begin to be understood by strangers more easily.

By 24–36 months

NON-VERBAL MILESTONES

- listens to and remembers simple stories with pictures
- understands three-word instructions such as 'where's my bag?'
- understands simple 'who', 'what' and 'where' questions.

VERBAL MILESTONES

- uses up to 300 words
- using more complex sentences with 4–5 words together, including adjectives and verbs, e.g. 'want more milk', 'she took my car', 'my red hat there', 'I falled down' (not able to use past tense properly)
- asks the name of things
- adds 's' to make plurals, even if that's not right. Using a general rule rather than imitation so will say 'trains' which is correct and 'mouses' which is not
- often has problems pronouncing words containing sh, ch, th and f
- plays with other children and shares things but still may do parallel play (where toddlers play side-by-side doing their own thing and not sharing)
- will stammer and stutter as she struggles to express herself.

Three and four years

NON-VERBAL MILESTONES

- can listen to longer stories and anecdotes and will ask and answer questions about what she has heard
- enjoys playing imagination games
- laughs at simple jokes and likes humour.

VERBAL MILESTONES

- answers simple questions about a picture book, e.g., 'Whose home did Goldilocks go to?'
- uses colours and numbers, e.g. 'green boat' and 'two apples'
- uses time-related adjectives such as 'yesterday' and 'tomorrow' though still may make mistakes
- able to answer questions about 'why' something has happened
- uses longer sentences and link sentences together
- describes events and activities that have already happened, e.g. 'we went park'
- tries to answer 'why' questions as well as asking 'what', 'where', and 'why' questions
- generalises past tense so may say 'runned' instead of 'ran'
- common to still mispronounce some words containing r, w, l, f, th, sh, ch and dz
- uses small numbers.

Language development problems

It can be very hard to spot if your child has a problem with communication and it's really important not to focus solely on vocabulary. Communication is about so much more than the number of words your toddler can use. Communication starts non-verbally, with that first lovely eye contact between you and your baby. Then, even before your baby can speak, she learns about taking turns in a conversation. Vitally, she learns to listen and attend to you and make a response; even if it's just to coo, smile or squeal.

If you are concerned that your toddler isn't talking, first assess her non-verbal communication. Does your toddler make eye contact with you? Does she smile? Does she listen? Does she respond, either non-verbally or with noises? If some or all of this communication behaviour is absent it's really important to get your toddler assessed professionally.

Try not to worry too much about mispronunciation and unclear speech as this is almost a defining factor of toddler speech. If you are really worried about anything about your toddler's speech which is quite different from her peers, speak to your health visitor or visit the I CAN website to help you compare your toddler's speech development to a range of milestones. Sometimes you just need to be patient and encourage the amazing process of language acquisition which takes many years.

Assessment by child development team

If you speak to your GP or health visitor, the first step they take is usually to arrange a hearing test. Even if your toddler does respond to noises during the tests, common conditions like glue ear can mean her hearing can come and go.

In the UK you can also self-refer your toddler to a speech therapist or get a referral via your health visitor. A speech therapist can:

- refer your toddler for a hearing test
- arrange a short speech therapy course
- support you to get your toddler a speech play worker if they attend a nursery.

Things that can help with delayed speech (depending on the underlying problem) include:

- getting grommets or treatment for hearing problems
- a speech therapy course
- signing up for a DVD or online course produced by a speech therapist to teach you how to help your toddler to communicate.

The chances are that your toddler will start talking perfectly in time. The good news is that even children with complex speech problems can get there eventually. You will be able to help your child by creating opportunities for speech, and by modelling language. These are things that a speech therapist will help you to learn.

There are several ways to encourage your child to talk. If you move things to where she doesn't expect you will create a need for her to ask. You could put toys in clear, sealed containers so she can see them and want them, but you don't give them to her until she makes a request. To begin with this could just be pointing, which is non-verbal communication; you build up her language skills by 'modelling' what she should say, e.g. 'animals?' 'want the animals?'

Another helpful technique with non-verbal toddlers is offering choice. Some toddlers' brains recognise words fairly easily but producing a word out of nowhere is quite hard. So, if your toddler wants a drink offer her a choice she can see, 'Do you want water or a hairbrush?' To make it even more straightforward you could also hold the actual objects as you offer them as options. Toddlers can pick this up quite quickly and it can cut down frustration levels immensely.

The transition from non-verbal baby to fluent school child is a miraculous development. In fact, communication and language development are so fundamental to this stage that toddlers could well be renamed 'talklers'. Your toddler's developing language will promote and enable her cognitive, social and emotional development – which we come on to in the next chapter.

YOUR TODDLER'S VOCABULARY

Language communication is about so much more than vocabulary. However, it is a good idea to have an idea of the words that your toddler uses.

By your toddler's second birthday she may know these words: Daddy, Mummy, more, hello, milk, juice, no, cat, dog, ball, eye, nose, car, shoe, hot, now, thank you.

These words will vary slightly from family to family, but they are some of the most important words to help her get by (a little like when you first visit a new country and you learn words to buy food). You may be the only person who can understand her pronunciation at first. These first nouns and instruction words are the building blocks that allow your toddler to communicate with you about her needs and the world around her. Her vocabulary can then begin to build rapidly, almost exponentially.

real parent story

Penny (Ellie, 4 years and Finn, 2 years)

'Ellie's speaking seemed to be like two steps forward and one step backwards. She'd make a new sound or a new word, say it constantly for a week and then it would be gone. I was obsessed with her knowing her colours and her numbers as she was my first, but I don't know if the rote learning really helped – luckily she loved her colours and counting books! By the time Finn came along I was more relaxed and just enjoyed chatting and sharing books.'

TEST: THE WUG TEST

The Wug Test was developed by Jean Berko Gleason to assess the generalised rules of grammar that English-speaking children apply as they learn to speak language. Different results are found in some other languages, such as Japanese when plurals are handled differently.

To try the test on your child you need to:

1. draw a picture of a nonsense item or animal
2. show the picture and say: 'This is a wug.'
3. show another identical picture and say, 'Now there is another one. There are two of them. There are two_____?

A child who says 'wugs' has never heard that word, but has used a grammar rule to form a plural.

Toddlers, in general, produce plurals to common words, e.g. 'cats' and 'dogs' at around 18 months old but they usually don't pass the wug test until around their third birthday.

TOP TIP

When you show your toddler a new thing with a new word, e.g. cow, talk about the cow in three different ways so your toddler notices and attends to the word cow. You will probably do this automatically!

emotional development

'This above all; to thine own self be true.'

William Shakespeare

Why is it that our earliest relationships leave such a lasting mark? A loving parent is not the norm in the animal kingdom. All animals produce babies but very few animal parents dedicate years to caring for their young like we do. Sea turtles, for example, lay hundreds of eggs and offer them no care other than a sandy nest. The fragile hatchlings are left to scramble down to the sea alone and very few survive to adulthood.

Mammals developed a different strategy that saw their babies kept safe inside the mother's body. However, even by mammalian standards we human parents are extremely loving. When our ancestors evolved big brains and stood up on two legs to walk, giving birth became more difficult, and our ancestors compromised by giving birth to premature and helpless babies. Our babies are born with an incompletely formed brain, which grows five-fold from birth to adulthood. This is why our babies need love and lots of care.

We usually only have one baby at a time and we love and care for them intensively, for not just days, but many years, whilst they grow to full adulthood. We literally teach them everything they know.

Unlike geese we don't attach or imprint instantly on our parents (or the first thing we see) at birth. Bonding for humans is a process that involves lots of physical and emotional proximity over time during which parent and child develop a deep emotional attachment.

Love and brain development

Can the love and nurture we experience as babies and toddlers really affect our brain development, potential and future? Your toddler's brain has over 100 billion special cells called neurons, each one of which can connect to as many as 7,000 other brain cells, and like other human brains, it's the most complicated object in the known universe! But a toddler's brain is also immature. The experiences a toddler has leads to multitudes of new connections in the brain. So yes, love, interaction and talking all promote your toddler's brain development.

Neurobiologists are reporting that parental love affects the brain, and lack of love has a long-term effect that lasts across generations. One key example is behaviour and how this is affected.

Studies of mice show that 'loving' mothers who are attentive and lick their babies, in turn had babies who were also good parents. This continued over at least two generations. It's good news all the way for the 'loved' mice. They also turn out to be:

- more intelligent than those that have been 'neglected'
- less aggressive
- more sociable.

It seems that these changes may be caused by chemical alterations in the genes and hormones in the brains of the baby mice – called 'epigenetic effects'.

Emotional regulation

Toddlers can feel the full spectrum of emotion, from desperate sadness, through fury, to joy in a matter of minutes. Part of your job as a parent is to help your toddler to control and regulate his emotions. This is because he does not yet have the mental hardware to do this for himself. Toddlers' emotions are like a central heating system and you as the parent work as their thermostat. Sometimes they need cooling down and sometimes they need warming up. Don't worry that this requires complicated skills – it doesn't. Regulating your toddler's emotions can be as simple but as powerful as:

- reassuring him when he is frightened
- calming him down when he is angry and has lost control
- cheering him up when he feels sad.

As your toddler becomes a pre-schooler and then a school-aged child he will begin to internalise the ability to regulate and manage his emotions and to understand where they come from.

Self-esteem

Your toddler's self-esteem has been built in the first year by having a warm, sensitive and loving bond with you and your partner. This secure attachment is the foundation and bedrock of your toddler's self-worth and resilience.

The way that you talk about your toddler's attributes, behaviour, body and personality now will begin the narrative that he holds inside himself of who he is.

Whilst a sense of being loved helps to promote your toddler's self-esteem, a study published in 2015 by the National Academy of Sciences warned against fostering narcissism (a term to describe extreme selfishness, with a grandiose view of the self and a craving for admiration) in your child. The study followed 565 children in the Netherlands. The children whose parents told them that they were 'more special than other children' and 'deserve something extra in life' were more likely to score highly for narcissism than the other children in the study. In contrast, those children who were told they were loved by their parents demonstrated higher self-esteem but not narcissistic attitudes. This study suggests that love and warmth are more effective at boosting your toddler's self-esteem than telling them they are special (in a universal sense).

Praising effort

Praising effort teaches children with natural abilities that they have a role in honing their skills and the things they love to do, which is both true and empowering. It is better to concentrate on praising your toddler's efforts rather than his 'abilities'. For example, if your toddler is persisting at a new task, praise his persistence rather than the ability. Get into the habit of saying 'well done, you keep trying to climb up the stairs don't you.' rather than 'you are the best at climbing stairs.' That way from an early age your toddler learns to understand that you appreciate and praise his persistence, tenacity and willingness to practise, which are crucial aspect of all learning. I know from personal experience that it's hard not to gush about your child's abilities to them, especially if they are gifted at something and doubt themselves. I have found myself telling my children: 'you are a natural at football.' The reason for this may be that children believe that they are a 'natural' at something, when the reality is that a huge part of what makes David Beckham a great footballer and The Beatles a great band is practice. In Malcolm Gladwell's wonderful book, *Outliers*, he explains the theory that most maestros in their field have dedicated 10,000 hours (over ten years of their life) to practising.

Body confidence

The chances are that your toddler will have inherited many of your physical traits; whether it's the shape of your toes, curly hair or height.

The lovely thing is that although you may not love some of these attributes in yourself you can learn to love and recognise them in your child. Here is a good opportunity to be kind to yourself and to your toddler. The more you can be joyful and enjoy your body for play, to eat, to run and splash, the more you will imbue your toddler with confidence and encourage their natural delight in their little bodies and what they can do.

The way you talk about your own body will have a big impact on your toddler, as he develops from an adorably unselfconscious baby to a pre-schooler with a vocabulary to describe what people look like. It can be quite a lot of baggage to unlearn, but the good news is that once you learn to use respectful and loving words about the bodies of you, your family and the people in your lives it really begins to change your own perspective. A new approach can help you to heal any negative attitudes that you may have picked up as a child.

I was hugely lucky to have a mum and dad with positive body images, who led active lives and enjoyed sports. I never heard them say anything negative about my body or their own bodies. They were not vain, just happy with their wonderful and healthy bodies. When I had the opportunity to discuss this with parents on Sky News Sunrise I realised how lucky I was and what a happy and positive body image I had compared to so many women. I hope and strive to pass this on to my daughters and my son and rather unusually it is my husband who looks in the mirror and complains about what he sees in our household but he is trying to be more compassionate to himself and the children (as they don't like to hear anyone being mean about their dad – even if it's him!).

The language you use around food, weight, bodies and beauty informs your toddler's vocabulary. Be kind and compassionate to yourself, your toddler and those people around you and he will too.

Using positive words such as 'strong', 'beautiful', 'graceful' and 'powerful' help people feel positive and the same power is there for negative words. Avoid using words like 'disgusting', 'pathetic' and 'gross'. Remember that your body and your toddler's body are natural miracles!

---

real parent story

Dee (Nelly, 18 months)

'I'm a terrible body checker. Every morning I have a ritual; I weigh myself in the bathroom and then use the full-length mirror to look at my bum and legs and usually sigh and say something about how big my bum is before pulling on my clothes and moaning at how tight my jeans are because of my big bum. My toddler is usually in the bathroom with me ... because mums never get to go to the loo by themselves! Anyway, like all toddlers, she copies everything so now she stands on the scales and harrumphs and looks in the mirror turning to see her bum in her little nappy. Though it was cute it really hit me that I didn't want her to dislike her lovely little body like I had learned to. So I made a change. I stopped weighing myself in front of her and checking out my bum in the mirror. I also tried to change my language about my body and talked about being strong and enjoying sports. I'm hoping she will copy this behaviour just as readily.'

Recognition of other people's emotions

Facial expressions are the same around the world and mean the same thing across cultures. This is because we all have the same facial muscles and the same instincts to make and comprehend facial expressions. Babies soon recognise that someone is frightened, without needing to have it explained to them. Did you know that a child's own facial expressions change their physiology; they feedback and amplify their own emotions. So when your toddler smiles, the muscles used for smiling *promote a reward* in his brain. When he pulls a disgust face, his brain responds as if feeling that emotion. The face and emotions are inextricably linked. Toddlers on the autism disorder spectrum may have a reduced ability to recognise emotions in other people (more on this in Chapter 6).

Empathy can be improved and developed in toddlers (and all people!); there is a wonderful TED ('Ideas Worth Spreading' website) talk showing how empathy can be improved, following empathy lessons in a Japanese school. If you would like to help your toddler's empathy from an early age, one idea is to be open about describing your emotions and acknowledging his feelings, e.g.: 'I know you are really sad that we had to leave the park and I'm sorry, but we will come back tomorrow.'

Milestones of emotional development

By 15 months

- still carries teddies upside down by arms
- throws down items in play.

By 18 months

- prefers solitary play
- says 'me do it' a lot
- tunes in to his parents' anxiety as they take risks
- occasional tantrums.

By 30 months

- impulsive and explores his environment
- probably has a tantrum each day

- will help as long as it doesn't prevent his plans
- will play with other children more but doesn't share his toys easily.

By 36 months

- starts to enjoy and take part in family meals
- 'looks after' younger siblings, pets and teddies
- cooperates with adults in tasks and chores
- knows if they are a boy or a girl
- has his first friend
- beginning to have theory of mind to see another person's point of view or feeling.

The power of routine

Chaotic schedules can make many toddlers much more likely to melt down as they lose a sense of what the next steps are. A routine for mealtimes, sleep and rest can really help toddlers to feel like the environment they are living in isn't out of control and overwhelming.

Toddlers are more likely to suffer with classic struggles like hunger, thirst, tiredness and overstimulation. Just as adults can get grumpy when tired and hungry, so can toddlers, of course, yet your toddler might not realise that is why he feels so fed-up.

Having a regular bedtime and a routine for getting ready for bed (see page 231), regular times for meals, and a ready supply of healthy snacks and water in between, will help your child cope with the demands of the day. A regular rest time is still important as your child gets older, especially if he has been out in the day, at nursery or playing with friends.

How to calm your toddler

Whilst it is completely normal for your toddler to get cross, sad, boisterous or even withdrawn, it is helpful to have some 'joker cards' ready to help your toddler to acknowledge how he feels and to calm down in an accepting environment. Calming activities can, and should, be part of every day, especially if your toddler has a tendency to get emotionally intense.

Music

Having a playlist of classical or contemporary tracks is a great way to gently stimulate and modulate your toddler's energy levels; some music is great for winding down at the end of the day or after a tiring activity. Whether you are at home, in the car, or out and about, a CD or your phone playlist can lift everyone's spirits.

If mornings are stressful, trying to leave home on time, why not have a particular tune to get ready to. It can be a lovely part of a routine to include music; for some reason our morning happy anthem when we are all getting ready to walk to school is a song by Jimmy Cliff. It has a calming and yet energising effect on the whole family; we are nicer to each other and we all trot round the house and get ready much more quickly and happily!

To help soothe the bedtime routine, there are some beautiful classical pieces such as Pachelbel's 'Canon in D Major' and 'Air on a G String' by Bach. Nothing beats parents singing lullabies; it might sound old-fashioned but a parent's voice is incredibly soothing. My children still ask me to sing them 'The Manx Lullaby' (which I like too as my family are a tiny bit Manx).

Rhythmic movement and dance

Parents and grandparents since the dawn of time have used natural physical movement to soothe children. Heartbeats and footsteps as we walk and carry our children mirror their own heartbeats and soothe, which is one reason why children love being carried. If you rock your toddler in your arms he will quickly focus on this movement and inadvertently move his attention away from his anger or sadness to return to a state of calm.

Art

Toddlers need lots of physical activity but they also really benefit from quiet, focused activities too. Finger painting, pavement chalking and any opportunities to play with colour, mark-making and art are popular, and can lead to quiet absorption.

Physical activity

Physical activity has a calming effect on all of us. When our bodies and minds are working together we feel more in sync and this has a knock-on effect on our physiology and emotions. Your toddler will benefit from the positive feedback of physical exertion and deep breathing. Being active outside is great as the fresh air can also help to boost overall calm and contentment.

Being in nature

Although many of us live urban lives, it is absolutely vital, in my opinion, that we let our toddlers commune with nature on a daily basis. The colour green is perhaps the most calming colour in the spectrum and spending time in green spaces, with grass and trees around can be very soothing. Toddlers have an innate love of natural history, for plants, animals, hills, pebbles, streams, rain, snow – take every opportunity to find, or create, an oasis of nature in your daily life for you and your toddler.

Instant calming activities

Calming activities can also be 'deployed' in the midst of a meltdown and these interventions will be more focused and one-to-one, allowing you to help bring your toddler back to a state of calm.

These 'fire-fighting' calming techniques include:

Using a calm voice

The importance of the tone and timbre of your voice as a parent cannot be overstated. You can say exactly the same sentence to your toddler and sound cajoling and panicked or calm and authoritative.

Your toddler will pick up on the emotion in your voice instinctively, so if you tend to get angry or anxious quickly in the midst of a toddler meltdown it is worth learning how to control your own reaction. Practise slowing your breathing, breathing from your abdomen (not shallow or 'thoracic' breathing). Speak calmly and with reassuring authority. The effect can be like a magic spell; your toddler will naturally slow down his breathing and once this process begins he will be better able to listen and respond rather than 'broadcast' his feelings outwards.

Calm touch

Feel confident in the power of your touch as a parent to soothe and calm your toddler. Whether you wrap him up in your arms for a cuddle or stroke his hair or back, your calm touch can soothe your child.

Side-tracking

Sometimes toddlers want a quick escape from the overwhelming emotion that has taken over their consciousness. Calling off his attention to something absurd or interesting can sometimes have an instantaneous effect and divert from the moment of tantrum. You will know what things are likely to be compelling and cheering to your toddler ('look at that cat!') and you will be amazed at what a powerful tool side-tracking is in your parent toolkit.

This tip comes with a caveat: your toddler's emotions are real so it is important to acknowledge your toddler's feelings with words. For example, if your toddler is cross about too much butter on his toast, you can say, 'I know that you are angry about the butter.' That's not to say that your toddler's emotions are not also sometimes absurd to us from the outside, but to him they are important.

Calm and toddler mindfulness

In some ways toddlers are utterly mindful; they truly live in the moment, in the zone. Your toddler experiences flow, i.e. he can be completely absorbed in the process of what he is doing without thinking about the end result or having an inner voice commenting on what he is doing and how he is succeeding or failing.

Mindfulness is about paying more attention to the present moment, to your thoughts, emotions and the world around you. Learning mindfulness techniques has been shown to improve mental well-being for adults and children.

There has been a welcome explosion of interest in recent years in how ancient mindfulness techniques like meditation can help us in our day-to-day lives. There is also an interest in mindfulness in nurseries and schools with support for troubled children. I find this 'mindfulness movement' hugely exciting and encouraging and think that the two best places to begin with mindfulness are:

a) when you become a parent and experience the seismic shift in calm and control in your own life
b) when your child becomes a toddler and his natural mindfulness can start to be replaced by increased self-reflection and anxiety. If we can help our toddlers to stay calm and mindful we can make their childhoods happier and their own developing minds calmer, more centred and balanced.

Whilst mindfulness is the natural state of toddlers, they can really struggle to keep calm if emotions are boiling over or if bored. Most toddlers will struggle to be still and quiet and cope with the boredom of not doing anything.

Here are ideas for naturally mindful activities that you can incorporate with your toddler and begin to make a habit of in his life. With these exercises you and your toddler can begin to make mindfulness a habit which can help you both to communicate with each other and notice yourself, your toddler and the world around you. This really comes very naturally to toddlers and you will find you learn a thing or two from them in the process!

Tasting

Take a juicy peach or a piece of chocolate each and describe and notice all the sensations as you very slowly eat it. Start by both smelling the food you are about to eat, then describe the texture and flavours as you taste. When your toddler is very young he may only be able to take part by listening to you and slowly eating his food but this is the first step in mindful eating.

Breathing

Toddlers are naturally good belly breathers but it can help to have a relaxation time, either during the day or before bedtime. Lie side-by-side with your hands on your bellies and breathe so that your hands rise up on your tummy and separate. Ask your toddler to breathe slowly and watch his belly rising and falling. Ask him to feel his hands heavy on his tummy. Count your breathing slowly up to ten; your breaths are naturally deeper than your toddler's so don't expect him to be able to breathe as slowly and deeply as you, but your breath will help his to slow and deepen.

Body consciousness

This technique is especially useful at bedtime, especially if your toddler is overtired or fidgety. In this classic relaxation technique ask your toddler to contract their muscles one at a time, first hard and then relax them. Start with the toes and feet and move up the body. It can be a bit of a challenge to know how to contract some muscles so simple instructions such as 'squeeze your hand into a fist as if you are squeezing out a sponge' or 'screw up your face' can help to explain.

Toddler massage

Don't think that baby massage has to end when your child becomes a toddler. Massage can be a lovely after-bath calming ritual. You can either massage over your toddler's pyjamas but for a more physically mindful massage use a gentle carrier oil suitable for toddlers (such as extra virgin olive oil).

Start with your toddler's feet, gently squeeze them in your hand and moving your hand from toes to heel, without tickling. Then do the same with your toddler's calves and thighs. The same techniques can be used on your toddler's hands and arms. When you massage your toddler's back or abdomen use gently fanning out movements like windscreen wipers with a gentle rotating movement. You can also gently stroke your toddler's tummy in a clockwise fashion which can help with digestion too.

Toddler massage should in no way be an extreme 'deep tissue' massage, instead stick to gentle baby massage techniques that focus on the sensations of your toddler's skin, without tickling which can be too intense and unbearable. Massage oil makes things less ticklish in general.

Never force a massage on your toddler; most toddlers will love a relaxing massage, but sometimes your toddler may be overstimulated or overtired and will not welcome it. Similarly some toddlers just generally find massage too overstimulating and you need to respect their preference; he might instead like to have his back stroked over his pyjamas.

Emojis

Toddlers are only just beginning to reflect on their emotions. Even before your toddler is able to articulate how he feels, it can help him to be mindful and recognise his emotions by talking about events of the day and the emotions you both felt around them. You might find it helps to print out some classic emojis of happy, sad, angry, surprised and scared faces. You and your toddler can point to the emojis that best describe how you both felt. This helps your toddler to recognise and notice their emotions which is a central part of mindfulness.

Emotional development problems

Toddlers need help from their parents to regulate their emotions; at the centre of this is their bond to you. If your toddler is 'securely attached' to you (as around 70 per cent of toddlers are), he will be more likely to develop independence and emotional resilience as he grows up. For this to happen toddlers need to feel unconditionally loved.

If you are concerned about the bond you have with your toddler (especially if you had a tough time after the birth and suffered with postnatal depression) there are lots of things you can do to support you and your toddler. Your toddler loves you unconditionally and doesn't judge you. You don't have to be Supermum or Superdad. Just spend lots of time chatting face-to-face with your toddler. Share books and cuddle while doing so. All these activities strengthen the bond and help to boost your confidence and happiness as well as that of your toddler. If you are worried, get support from your health visitor or GP who will be able to tell you of local services to support parents or it can be worth investing in counselling sessions for yourself, which can be more affordable than you think.

If you feel that your toddler is behind in the emotional developmental milestones (see above) or doesn't connect with you emotionally or seems emotionally withdrawn speak to your GP or health visitor. If your toddler seems to misbehave a lot or be violent, talk to your GP or health visitor.

---

real parent story

Fatima (Tariq, 2½ years)

'When Tariq turned two, the meltdowns came like clockwork. He used to throw himself on the floor in anger and sadness so often that I learned to react quickly and catch him. It put me off going to playgroups for a while but usually if I cuddled him and stroked the back of his neck he'd calm down and be completely back to happy.'

Body confidence

Toddlers display a wonderful body confidence; they love what their body can do and they all seem to stroke their little egg-shaped bellies with pride and delight. Sadly, after this peak of body confidence some children learn that bodies can be disappointing, disgusting, fat and un-loveable. This is such a tragedy and leads to low body confidence which can be transferred from one generation to the next. The good news is that with a few changes in the words you use about yourself and how you interact with your toddler you can prevent body hang-ups being passed on.

Quiz: Parent body confidence

1. This quiz looks at how you view yourself. Do you see yourself in a positive way? When you look at your reflection in the mirror do you:
   a) Groan, pull at bits of your face or body you don't like, and announce how 'fat', 'ugly' or 'terrible' you look?
   b) Spend a lot of time checking yourself in the mirror but only complain on bad days.
   c) Use the mirror briefly and don't make negative comments about yourself. Sometimes I might even say something positive.

2. How do you explain your exercise to your child?
   a) I treat exercise like a chore and say that I have to do some exercise as I'm so 'flabby', 'hideous' and 'out of shape'.
   b) I quite like exercise but will often explain that I need to lose some weight before, say, a wedding or holiday.
   c) I enjoy exercise and explain that it's good to be strong and fast.

3. Do you have physical play with your toddler?
   a) No, when we get to the park or an activity that's my chance to kick back and rest with a coffee and a magazine while she runs herself ragged.
   b) I will sometimes play if I'm begged but generally try and get out of it.
   c) One of the best things about having a child is it gives me an excuse to jump into pools, play at the park, and run around like a child – my toddler keeps me fit!

4. How do you talk about food?
   a) I talk about food in polarised terms; there is good, healthy food and bad, naughty food that will make me fat.
   b) I try to educate my toddler about good food and bad food and explain that some food makes you fat.

c) Food is both a fuel and a joy. I am very enthusiastic about a huge range of food and explain that our body needs food as fuel and we need to listen when it tells us that our body is hungry or full. I like to encourage my toddler to try all the foods I love.

5. Do you discuss other people's bodies with your toddler?
   a) I often say to friends: 'have you lost weight?' I also comment on their hair, clothes, skin – you name it!
   b) I always compliment people if they have made an effort.
   c) I like to boost people's confidence but don't just focus on the body. I'm just as likely to tell them they have a lovely voice or that they've been really kind than say anything about their appearance.

6. How do you discuss your toddler's body?
   a) I'm really worried about him gaining too much weight so I already limit his portions and tell him that he 'doesn't want to get fat' or 'get a big tummy'.
   b) I tell my toddler he's beautiful all the time and say he's going to be a supermodel when he grows up.
   c) My toddler's body is amazing, strong and fast. His skin is soft like a peach and his eyes are lovely. My toddler enjoys his amazing body and I spend as much time talking about his other attributes and interests.

7. How do you discuss your shared characteristics?
   a) My toddler knows I hate my curly hair and straighten it whenever I go out. He has curly hair too.
   b) We both have the same bottom but I've told him if he exercises it might not get as big as mine.
   c) One of the ways I've fallen in love with my body is seeing the shared characteristics in my daughter. I show her our shared features in the mirror, for example: 'Look! Our eyes are the same colour of green and you have freckles on your nose too!'

Mostly As: You seem to have low body confidence and perhaps without realising you are transferring lots of negative ideas about your body, your child's body and the role of food and exercise in our lives. Try to be kind to yourself. Ban yourself from criticising your body and try to enjoy a healthy balanced diet and activities with your toddler.

Mostly Bs: Like many people you have your ups and downs when it comes to your body. You probably had your body confidence knocked as a child and are trying to make sure it doesn't happen to your toddler. Try to be kind to yourself and your toddler and not focus so much on how your bodies look; instead, focus on what your bodies can do. Learn to reconnect with your lost love of physical activity and nourishing food.

Mostly Cs: You probably had parents who instilled a strong sense of body confidence in you with lots of activity and fun rather than focusing on appearance. You are pretty happy with your body and love to see your characteristics appearing in your toddler as he learns to walk, run and jump.

TOP TIP

Bonding is a long process and not a one-off event at birth, so don't panic that it's too late for you and your toddler to bond if you've struggled in the past.

chapter five

cognitive development

'If you want your children to be intelligent, read them fairy tales. If you want them to be more intelligent, read them more fairy tales.'

Albert Einstein

Toddlers do not think the way we think. Full stop. This is key to understanding your toddler. If you understand your toddler and how she looks at the world, you can guide and encourage her in a way that engages her developing brain. The study of cognitive development attempts to tease apart and understand how thinking changes and develops from birth to adulthood. Cognition or thinking includes:

- information processing
- conceptual thinking
- perception and integration of information from the senses (understanding the physical world around)
- use of language to think.

In other words, cognitive development is the emergence of the ability to think and understand.

Your toddler's cognitive development or thinking skills accelerate with help from her physical development. Being able to cruise or walk, reach for items and manipulate objects in her hand with her fine motor skills, opens up the world to your toddler by allowing her to approach, assess, perceive and experiment with new objects.

Talking and communicating with other people allows your toddler to 'stand on the shoulders of giants' and:

- conceptualise the physical and social world
- understand concepts explained by others
- understand and empathise increasingly with other people.

Toddler curiosity

Toddler curiosity knows no bounds. As your toddler glories in her increasing mobility and reach she will be into everything; opening cupboards and rooting in your bag. In order to facilitate this natural curiosity, have lots of interesting items at toddler height. Toddlers seem to especially like the illicit frisson of exploring something 'grown-up', so one idea would be to have one cupboard containing plastic boxes that she can safely explore. Plastic boxes are safe, lightweight items that your toddler can pull out, stack up and, of course, knock over. You might want to put child locks on cupboards that you don't want her opening! Brightly coloured objects like dishwasher tablets are very appealing to toddlers so keep them in a high cupboard as they are dangerous.

TOP TIP: GET DOWN TO YOUR TODDLER'S LEVEL

It's really important to get down to your toddler's level in order to see the world from her point of view. This way you can toddler-proof your home and be aware in the places you visit. Don't leave lighters or medicines in your bag on the floor as toddlers will not realise that these items are dangerous. Even small coins and batteries can end up in mouths.

Problem-solving and persistence

Faced with a problem your toddler will try one solution and then another. Toddlers can be very persistent, and although she may get frustrated, she doesn't yet tend to feel low self-esteem as she struggles with new problems. This makes toddlers tenacious, natural scientists. For example, if your toddler is playing with a shape sorter toy, she will try one solution and then another to find a matching hole. A few meltdowns when her attempts to solve a problem are thwarted are entirely normal; just be on hand to calm and encourage. If you can, try not to do it for her, instead let her work it out for herself with a little guidance.

Toddlers have a natural developing interest and innate understanding of the physical world. Even as babies they understand that our world has gravity and are confused if items defy gravity (for example, floating bubbles). Through play with liquids and solids toddlers refine their understanding of matter and cause-and-effect. Toddlers use their body to immerse themselves in real world experiments, such as splashing in water, knocking things over and enjoying being on swings and slides at the park. Encouraging all these activities will promote your child's natural curiosity and help boost her confidence.

By three years of age your toddler will understand there are living and non-living things in the world. At first it will be basic and often be down to whether something has a face, so a mushroom may not be defined as living but a robot dog might. Toddlers love to observe animals, so if you don't have pets take your toddler to visit farms or walk in the countryside to see animals. Toddlers are interested in the weather and how the outside world changes with the seasons and weather conditions so get your wellies on in the rain, play in the snow and splash around on the beach.

People, emotions and life lessons are probably the key interest of toddlers. This is where we begin to see differences in toddlers with autism as their 'social blindness' becomes increasingly apparent when other toddlers attend so tenaciously to the emerging social and emotional information around them. The best way you can harness and develop your toddler's natural interest in people and their emotions is simple – spend lots of time chatting to your toddler with full eye contact. In this

intimate arena your toddler is learning and beginning to understand how other people tick.

Play is a universal part of children's lives whatever culture,
tribe or time in history they come from. A lot of play focuses
on understanding and learning domestic skills such as cooking,
washing and DIY (see chapter seven on the importance of play).

Growing number skills

From your toddler's first birthday she will love to count up in
twos, such as 'one, two hands'; 'one, two eyes'. She will enjoy
actions songs that include counting that allow her to visualise
items such as, 'Three little ducks went swimming one day'. By
the age of two your toddler may have memorised counting to ten
but this is more a feat of language and memory than numeracy.

There are many opportunities to count with your toddler
and this will help to reinforce the idea of when you add one
thing to a group, the entire number goes up. Count out spoons
when you set the table and count flowers in a vase by physically
pointing at each one. Try to keep this as a fun game rather than
trying to make your toddler write down or identify numbers.
My autistic nephew loved to line up long lines of numbers from
an early age, so if your toddler is drawn to numbers and counting you can try lots of number games.

Sorting and classification skills

Sorting and classification is a hugely important human skill
which allows you to understand the world around you, for
example, animals versus plants, babies versus adults, wasps
versus ladybirds.

As your toddler's language acquisition accelerates, her ability
to sort and classify the world around her will become increasingly
sophisticated. Toddlers really enjoy sorting games, and again, this

is something that you can do as part of everyday life. For example, 'Let's sort the clothes into whites and colours before they go in the washing machine.' Even before your toddler can identify colours, she will be trying to make sense of categories that you are making. If you are playing with coloured shapes, she will observe that a red triangle might sometimes be sorted with the red things when you are sorting by colour, but it might go in with the triangles when you are sorting circles and triangles. Sorting games with two options makes it easier for your toddler to understand the category archetypes that are being sorted, which will encourage her. If this becomes too easy, move on at her pace.

GAMES TO PLAY WITH YOUR TODDLER

Here are some simple ideas of games to play that help to stimulate your toddler's thinking. Most just use items you will have in the home or that you will spot as you go about your usual routine.

Science games

These games show your toddler more about the world she lives in. There is so much magic in the physical world and the games below might help you to reveal and illustrate the physical properties of the world and the objects your toddler discovers in everyday life.

MELTING GAME

See how long it takes for an ice cube to melt placed on a plate on a sunny windowsill.

SCALES

If you have a set of old weighing scales, or can find one in a charity shop, let your toddler experiment with what weighs more. Take a tangerine and weigh it against an orange or your shoe compared to both your toddler's shoes.

ESTIMATING GAME

Ask your toddler (this might work best in older toddlers) to estimate how many potatoes will fit in a bowl as you prepare food. She can estimate and then count the potatoes to see if she was right. It is easier to estimate with small numbers, e.g., 'can you fit two teddies in your bag or just one?'.

SINK OR FLOAT GAME

A good game for bathtime. Choose five items with your toddler (perhaps a stick, stone, orange, cork and sponge) to take to the bathroom and test. Ask which she thinks will sink and which will float and let her experiment.

SEE-THROUGH, SOLID OR REFLECTION GAME

Collect and compare various objects that might be see-through, solid or reflective. This could include a sheet of paper, sweet wrappers, a mirror, tracing paper. Even if your toddler isn't able to articulate the properties of these materials they will like to explore and look at the different materials. You can say 'I can see you!' looking through a coloured sweetie wrapper and play together with the mirror to look at each other's faces and play peek-a-boo.

COLOUR GAMES

Explore what happens to colours when mixed together. You could try using coloured bath 'bombs' or paints, encouraging your toddler to mix them together; red and blue mixed together create purple, blue and yellow make green, red and white make pink, and red and yellow make orange.

Sorting games

These games help your toddler understand the concept of size, colour and other categories.

DOING SOMETHING WRONG GAMES

Toddlers love it when you do something silly or wrong and will enjoy the 'audience participation' of shouting 'No!' See what she does when you try to put her socks on her hands. 'Negation' games help your toddler to understand basic concepts about how the world works; she has so many conceptual rules to understand and humour can really boost her confidence and make her feel grown up and knowledgeable. It is just fun too.

ANIMAL, VEGETABLE OR NON-LIVING GAME

Teach and assess whether your child understands the concept of living and non-living things. If you are out and about on a walk you can ask your toddler whether various things are alive, for example, the slide, a cat you walk past, flowers on the pavement, a moving bus. Initially, simple rules like 'things that move are alive' or 'things with faces are alive' might be the first concepts your toddler holds in her head. Over time her concept of what is living will become more sophisticated so that she understands that a robot dog is not the same as a living dog, even though it has a face and moves. That said, it is perfectly normal to have a global 'anthropomorphic' attitude to some non-living things and treat them as alive, such as the family car. It is probably a side effect of our huge potential for empathy and interest in living things.

SORTING AND MAKING GROUPS GAME

Take a collection of same-sized objects, such as wood blocks or cotton reels, and ask your toddler to sort them into piles according to colour or size, or other category. These categorisation skills will improve over time and will start with your toddler just having the opportunity to observe the variety.

FOOD SPOTTING GAME

Categorise and spot food based on its colour and size. Older toddlers might also enjoy working out whether it's a fruit, vegetable, leaf or from an animal. You can play this game at home with fresh food or even toy food but it can be lovely to explore all the variety at a fruit and vegetable stall and maybe decide you will buy 'three red things' and choose together, e.g. a red apple, a punnet of strawberries and a bag of tomatoes.

MATCH THE PARENT GAME

Collect photos of animals. Ask your toddler to put the baby animals with their parents. Start with domestic animals, then farm animals and try an example where the parent and baby do not resemble each other (for example, a butterfly and caterpillar).

OPPOSITES GAME

Look for opposites in books and when you are out and about. For example, push the buggy or scooter backwards and forwards, or pick up big footballs and small tennis balls. This helps your toddler begin to understand these adjectives (describing words).

- tall – short
- living – non-living
- old – young
- big – small
- empty – full
- rough – smooth
- dark – light
- forwards – backwards
- hot – cold
- over – under

Sound and music games

As well as being good fun, sound and music games help your toddler experiment with different materials and sounds, and also understand cause-and-effect.

MUSICAL INSTRUMENTS AND BOTTLE ORCHESTRA

Create musical instruments with items from your home and garden and let your toddler shake and bang on them to make sounds. Plastic bottles can provide lots of instruments. Fill bottles with different amounts of water and blow across the neck of the bottle to hear its unique sound. Which bottles (with deep or shallow water) produce the highest and deepest notes? You can also fill bottles with different items (for example, rice or pistachio shells) and re-seal the top. Your toddler will love the sound, sight and feel of the rice or nut shells sliding up and down the bottle.

SOUND COPYING GAME

Ask your toddler to listen and match the sounds that you make. You could imitate farmyard animals and sounds from around the home. Remember to take turns and let her choose some sounds for you to try and copy.

WHISPER, TALK AND SHOUT GAME

Can your child copy you when you whisper, speak or shout? Can she describe whether you are whispering, speaking or shouting?

Social and emotional development games

FACE GAMES

Toddlers are fascinated by faces and expressions and have an innate capacity to read and pull faces. Using your face and hers, you can play lots of fun games together that help her to understand faces and the emotions they can convey.

There is evidence that boys (in general) have more trouble reading facial emotions than girls of the same age. This is particularly true of boys (and girls) on the Autism Disorders spectrum. These games may be particularly helpful in this case.

WHAT ARE THEY FEELING GAME

Can your toddler describe what the babies, children and adults are feeling in a picture book by looking at their facial expressions and listening to the story? For example, if the duckling is lost, how did she feel do you think? How would you feel if you were lost?

MEMORY GAMES

Can your older toddler remember and match pairs? There are some beautiful, compelling designs available, and toddlers love to try and concentrate and remember; young children can have a very good memory, especially spatial memory.

Start with two pairs of picture cards. Place all the cards face down on a low table. Take turns with your child to turn over two cards. If the cards match the person who selected the pair keeps them and gets a clap or a cheer. Add in more pairs as she gets better at remembering where the cards are.

Milestones of cognitive development

Here is an overview of the order and timing of major milestones in how your toddler thinks. Remember, there is always a normal range around these average timings with half reaching the milestone earlier than average and half meeting the milestone later than average

By 15 months
- understands your words for some body parts, e.g. head
- points to several pictures of familiar nouns, e.g. dog
- understands the words 'no' and 'look'
- seeks out a hidden toy by moving things out of the way or going to where it fell.

By 18 months
- can point to her body parts when asked, e.g., 'Where is your arm?'
- favourite word to say is often 'no!'
- has a vocabulary of between 5 and 40 words
- gestures with arms to communicate excitement, e.g. 'more', 'do it again'
- points and ejaculates urgent words
- can carry out simple instructions, e.g. 'bring the teddy here'
- refers to herself with her name (or a garbled version)
- likes simple matching and sorting games and jigsaws
- starting to enjoy mark-making
- uses gestures and a few nouns to tell you what she wants
- she can copy your actions
- her memory is improving so she can remember things that happened a week ago
- doesn't respond with anger yet if a toy is taken away
- cannot see things from another person's perspective
- has no self-recognition so if you put a red sticker on her forehead and show her her reflection she will not touch the sticker (see page 92).

By 24 months
- has a vocabulary of 200 words, mainly nouns
- leaves the ends and beginnings of words, e.g. bag sounds like 'ba'
- may understand over 1,000 words
- refining understanding of cause and effect, e.g. when she blows on a candle and it goes out

- uses comforting words and gestures if a baby cries
- can follow more complicated instructions, e.g. 'bring me the nappy bags from my bag'
- developing self-recognition, e.g. identifies themselves in the mirror and in photos
- starting to put words together
- working things out in her head without trial and error
- goes back to find things where they last were
- enjoys pretend play and imitating
- snatches back a toy taken away.

By 30 months
- knows her full name
- asks 'who' and 'what' questions
- uses 'I', 'me' and 'you'
- likes construction toys such as Lego or Duplo.

By 36 months
- knows the primary colours
- asks 'why' questions
- understands number concept of 'one' and 'lots'
- can categorise and sort items, e.g. sort blocks into three colour groups.

Cognitive development problems

By looking at the milestones of cognitive development above you will have a rough idea of how your toddler should be thinking, conceptualising and playing during the toddler years. It can be hard to know how your toddler is thinking and conceptualising by looking at their outside behaviour but here are a few pointers to look out for:

1st birthday check
By 12–18 months your toddler should make full eye contact and smile and laugh with you and respond to her name when you

call it out. She should point to things that interest her and play with a range of toys.

2nd birthday check

Displays pretend play, e.g. using a banana as a telephone and doesn't interact with you or others during play, e.g. looking to you for a reaction or showing you toys. When sharing books she should be pointing and labelling some nouns in the book, e.g. dog (even if not clearly said).

3rd birthday check

By her third birthday your toddler should be able to follow two- or three- part instructions, e.g. 'please find your tooth-brush and clean your teeth'. She should be able to answer simple questions and tell you about her physical needs, e.g. thirsty, tired.

TOP TIP

It's really important to be your toddler's advocate and to speak to your GP or health visitor if you have concerns about any developmental delay. Early intervention by you and a child development team can be crucial to supporting your toddler's development, and can help to provide her with any extra help she needs to fulfil her potential.

real parent story

Lesia (Kai, 30 months)

'Kai is a proper little busybody. Every walk to the shops takes ages, he picks up everything, touches spider webs, put his hands in puddles. He reminds me of ET, on a new planet and checking out the world like a proper little scientist. Bless.'

SELF-RECOGNITION TEST

By 24 months your toddler should begin to develop self-recognition. So if you put a red sticker on her forehead and show her her reflection, she will realise that the reflection is her. She should realise that this means the sticker is on her forehead, and will reach up to touch or remove it.

TOP TIP

Talk to your toddler and give her plenty of time to respond – this is the most crucial way you can connect with your toddler and help her to make cognitive leaps.

chapter six

toddlers with special needs

'Everybody is a genius. But if you judge a fish by its ability to climb a tree, it will live its whole life believing that it is stupid.'

Albert Einstein

It is often during the toddler years that parents first worry that their toddler may be developmentally delayed. They see other toddlers walking, talking and interacting with their parents differently. Most parents, at one time or another, will worry or despair that their toddler seems behind or different. So how do you know if your concerns have grounds or if you are just being a worrier?

It's important that if a parent feels concern about their toddler's development it is taken seriously and checked out. False reassurance isn't helpful and you as the parent are the world expert on your own toddler.

If you are worried about some aspect of your toddler's development, speak to your GP or health visitor. Take a list of observations you have made, and maybe a video, if you think it will help, e.g. showing your toddler using one side of his body more than the other. The GP or health visitor may refer your toddler to the local child development team to be assessed. Try not to worry about this. Either the team will be able to reassure you, or they will be able to offer suggestions that will help support and promote your toddler's development.

If you feel you are not getting the help you need you can contact a national support group or charity; for example, if you think your toddler isn't talking or hearing well you could contact the I CAN children's charity (see page 47).

The autism spectrum

It is in the toddler years that many parents begin to worry about 'autism spectrum disorders' (ASD); a condition that can affect social interaction, communication, interests and behaviour. The spectrum includes Asperger's syndrome (AS). In the UK, 1 in 100 people will have an ASD and statistics from the United States report that around 1 in 70 children are diagnosed with ASD. This formal diagnosis doesn't usually happen until after the age of two years old. Researchers like Simon Baron-Cohen at Cambridge University and Amil Klin have developed assessments that can pick up signs of ASD in much younger babies and toddlers. Baron-Cohen states that the differences between Asperger's syndrome (which is sometimes called 'high-functioning' autism) and autism is that autistic children generally have language delay and below average IQ. Children with Asperger's syndrome are more likely to have above average IQs and no language delay.

Early diagnosis and intervention can help an autistic child to learn coping skills, so it is important to be aware of your toddler's development. Some classic behaviours to look out for include shrieking, lining up toys and stimming (see below). There is a wide range of behaviour in the spectrum, and every child is unique, so a child with ASD may share some, or all of the following behaviours.

Notice if your toddler is beginning to display repetitive behaviours or compulsive behaviours, particularly if she gets very distressed when prevented from carrying out the behaviour.

All children have their own idiosyncrasies so it is not to say this is diagnostic in itself, but may point to autism, or at least help you to understand how your child is thinking.

TOP TIP

It can seem really daunting to go down the route of having your precious child labelled as 'special needs' or having an Education, Health and Care Plan (HEC). Try to think of this as giving her a gateway to more help and support, which will result in many of her needs being met rather than glossed over.

Some early clues that parents might notice include:

Smiling

Full-term babies will make full eye contact and smile in response to your smile, from around six weeks old. Autistic children do smile and laugh but it can often be an 'unshared' smile. If your baby isn't smiling in response to your smile or laugh by six months you should talk to your GP.

Imitation

Can your toddler copy a happy or sad face? The human face has 43 facial muscles and can display seven clear emotions: anger, sadness, fear, surprise, disgust, contempt and happiness. Babies are able to pull sad faces from birth and happy, smiling faces soon afterwards. Human beings have an instinctive understanding of other people's facial emotions, and even non-verbal babies will react with caution if their mum displays a fearful face. It seems that our facial emotions are a window to our internal feelings and if we see sad anguish on someone's face we feel a strong empathy for them. Toddlers are fascinated by faces and study them with extreme concentration. You can begin by pulling a range of faces and matching them to the words for those emotions and then you can ask your toddler to copy you and pull the same face. Frequently in picture books the characters have exaggerated facial emotions that help to tell the story.

Autistic children are less likely to make eye contact and to look at your face. This feeds into a lack of imitation and, therefore, empathy. This means that a child may be less able to understand people's motivations and internal states. As our language is so multi-faceted, a child with ASD might have a completely literal understanding of what people say and how they act; so if a sibling says sarcastically: 'oh the cakes you made are delicious', the child will assume that their brother or sister really thinks the cakes are delicious. Sarcasm and lies can be lost on them.

If you have noticed from around nine months that your baby doesn't take part in turn-taking with you or copy what you do speak to your GP.

Babbling and cooing

Babbling is something that babies from all cultures and language backgrounds do. Babies in China babble in an identical way to babies in Iceland or Borneo. Babies begin to babble from about four months of age with classic 'baa baa daa daa' noises. It can be something babies do while on their own too, and you may hear your baby babbling away in her cot or while kicking about on a mat.

The human language instinct is incredibly powerful and mind-boggling. Early cooing and babbling are vital first steps where babies make a standard repertoire of noises with their mouth and vocal cords and hear themselves making all those noises.

If you notice that your baby didn't make cooing or babbling noises by the time she is six months old, or the babbling was delayed or sounds different to other babies, it's really important to speak to your GP.

Attention-seeking

We frequently praise toddlers who can amuse themselves for long periods of time. However, attention-seeking behaviour is actually a really important part of a child's social and emotional development. When a toddler uses you as her secure base, she explores and comes back to you, looks at your face for a reaction and indicates when to be picked up, this is all vital 'attention-seeking' behaviour. It is about sharing time and space with her primary caregiver and monitoring her emotions..

If you notice that your toddler rarely tries to get your attention or share a moment, it may be a sign that she struggles to relate to other people in a straightforward way, and it is worth discussing this with your GP.

Pointing and gesturing

Before spoken language there is a huge amount of communication that happens with body language and gesturing. You will realise the power of this form of communication if you have ever been in a country where you cannot speak the language. It is amazing how much you can communicate with facial expression, smiles and simple gestures. Before their first birthday babies generally wave 'bye bye', point, or gesture to be picked up.

Pointing is particularly interesting, because it is asking a person to look and notice what they are pointing at. It seems simple, but it is a huge jump in cognitive development. It means your toddler realises that another individual doesn't automatically share their literal or emotional point of view. Try to notice how and when your toddler gestures. If you notice that your toddler doesn't point or try and get your attention by the age of 15 months it's really important to speak to your GP.

Repetitive or stereotypic behaviours

Some children on the autism spectrum display repetitive behaviours which are thought to calm them when they feel overloaded with information. This is called 'stimming' or self-stimulation. It can include running up and down in a straight line, flapping their wrists, spinning, or sometimes more troubling behaviours like head-banging.

In my family, my siblings and I each have a child who loves to stim by running up and down. If all three of them are at their grandparents' home, it is funny to see each of them choose their little route and run up and down with a look of complete concentration or joy on their face. Only one of the three children is autistic and I wonder what it means about the possible genetic predisposition in our family to these behaviours. This is not copying behaviour but seems to be a shared trait. I ask my daughter what she's thinking about when she has a stimming session and she usually says she's having a fun imagination thought, as if it somehow helps her to process and think. All children display foibles and idiosyncrasies and it's important to see the big picture for each child and whether overall they are finding social interaction challenging.

Lack of reaction to her name

We are primed to notice and react to our name being called out. Chances are, if you hear your name called out or mentioned in a busy restaurant you will look up and try and spot the person who spoke.

From about seven months babies begin to respond and look up when their name is spoken. A lack of response to their name can be an early sign of autism. If there is a lack of reaction to your voice, particularly if you are out of your baby or toddler's peripheral vision this can, of course, also be a sign of hearing problems, so it may be important to have your toddler's hearing tested in the first instance. However, if your baby or toddler seems to respond to noises but doesn't react especially to her name, discuss this with your GP or health visitor.

POOR EYE CONTACT

Films like *Rain Man* and *Mercury Rising* have meant that limited eye contact is probably one of the most well-known signs of autism. But why is lack of eye contact such a key sign?

Some autistic children find direct eye contact overwhelming, and some autistic people do not respond to eye contact as they don't seem to recognise the important communication between two people making eye contact.

Eye contact and following eye direction is so important to human communication that some evolutionary biologists have postulated that this is the reason that human beings (unlike other animals) have eye whites. With the evolution of the whites of eyes around our irises, we are able to accurately assess *where* another human being is looking from a considerable distance.

One of the most fascinating and enlightening things I have ever read about people with autism was a study carried out by Amil Klin and told by Malcolm Gladwell in his book *Blink*. Klin invited autistic adults to watch the film *Who's Afraid of Virginia Woolf?*; a film full of double meanings and knowing looks.

This film was a complete mystery to Klin's subjects because they were unable to understand the subtext. Not only that, but they didn't treat the human face as something special to attend to, that can give out vast amounts of information about the person.

When one very bright Asperger's participant was monitored watching a particularly intense scene, Gladwell reported that the man spent more time looking at the light switch in the scene than he did looking at the faces of Richard Burton and Elizabeth Taylor! He was 'mind blind' and could only process a literal understanding of words exchanged to understand a person's internal feelings. Sarcasm and passive aggressiveness would be lost on him. Imagine trying to understand the complex world of human interaction if you were mind blind.

Severe lack of eye contact in your toddler can be a sign of autism; children on the autistic spectrum are more likely to look at moving objects. If you are trying to attract your toddler's attention to your facial expressions it can help to remove other distractions; their tendency to be distracted gives her less opportunity to see expressions and learn about them. So don't try to talk to her with the television going in the background because she won't tune it out. It can also help to have a series of signals before you speak to your toddler, e.g. say your toddler's name, then say 'look', and accompany the word look with a sign for look, e.g. index finger and middle finger pointing at each of your eyes.

DELAYED PHYSICAL DEVELOPMENT

Some autistic children have delayed milestones in their physical development, such as crawling and rolling, largely because autism is very often diagnosed alongside other conditions, such as dyslexia, dyspraxia, attention-deficit hyperactivity disorder (ADHD) and learning disabilities. However, in the case of my nephew, he was a very early walker and hit his physical milestones early. In a way we thought of him as a 'walker not a talker' as we had noticed that the early talkers in our extended family were later walkers and the early walkers were later talkers.

It's always worth speaking to your GP if you have noticed that your toddler was very late in her physical milestones as it may indicate an underlying problem (not just autism) and early intervention is always better.

There is a very strong culture in parenting today (from parents, psychologists and extended family) of reassurance and acceptance of toddlers' development and milestones. This relaxed environment helps save parents from worrying needlessly over minor differences in their toddler's development.

However, false reassurance is ultimately not helpful to parents and certainly not to the toddler with autism. Early intervention can make a huge and positive difference to your toddler and your ability to relate to them and help them develop.

However, don't be complacent as this culture of reassurance can extend into the healthcare professionals. My nephew has autism and had severe glue ear. On his first visit to the GP his mum was told his language delay was just because he was a 'lazy boy', he would speak later. It took some time for his mum to go to health professionals again with the same concern. The health visitors did respond. Health visitors can refer children to speech therapy services, indeed parents can self-refer to speech therapy services. The speech therapists picked up the problem straight away and showed concern at how far behind my nephew was. They are specialists in language development and can give clear information about whether there is a problem or not. There were further hurdles; when my nephew was finally referred to an ENT consultant the doctor said although there was glue ear the real problem was that he had a dummy – so he recommended a 'wait and see' approach. Subsequent ENT consultants were thankfully not so complacent about this language development and hearing and the glue ear was sorted out.

TOP TIP

There are many amazing healthcare professionals working in our communities. GPs and health visitors have good general knowledge but they may not have much specific experience with autism. Hopefully they can refer you to specialist teams as quickly as possible. If you, as the parent, are convinced your child needs extra support and your GP is at first dismissive, you can seek a second opinion or ask advice from an external charity.

How to get help

Your toddler will already have had regular assessments of her development and these should continue in the toddler years.

The first year
Between 9 and 12 months your health visitor will talk to you about your baby and assess their development. This is a good time to discuss any concerns you have and talk about any developmental milestones that are delayed or absent. Sometimes you will be given a development questionnaire to complete.

One to three years
At 30 months (around two and a half years) your health visitor should carry out another review of your toddler's development (things can be a little different from local authority to local authority so make sure you are attending reviews and ask for a meeting if you want to discuss your toddler's development and there is no assessment due). You can have quick discussions at your local well baby clinic but it's best to arrange a proper meeting if you want to discuss things properly. Also if your toddler attends a nursery their assessment might be done there along with their early years progress check at age two.

The review should include physical, cognitive, language and emotional/social development, including hearing, speech, social skills and behaviour.

The development review is partly designed to identify if your toddler may have an autistic spectrum disorder. If problems are identified then your toddler can be referred to your local Child Development Unit (CDU). The team of health professionals working in these centres have a wealth of experience in all kinds of development delays and problems and include paediatricians, educational psychologists and speech therapists.

It is the role of the CDU to determine and coordinate the help you and your toddler will need. You may be offered:

- toddler talk groups
- speech therapy training for parents
- special needs dentists (experienced with reluctant or frightened children)
- specialist assessment
- hearing tests
- individual speech therapy support
- play visitors.

---

real parent story

Katie (Ivan, 4 years)

'Parenting a child with special needs is demanding. Get the support that is available to you. Your child will develop and you will celebrate each bit of progress. Last week we were cheering because my son's autistic classmate had told her first lie. Theory of mind! The speed and direction of the development of a child with special needs will be individual, as it should be for every child anyway.'

Quiz: Might my toddler be on the autism spectrum?

These questions will help you formulate whether you feel that your toddler may be displaying some signs and symptoms of autism spectrum disorder. It is in no way a diagnosis, but may help you to decide whether to speak to your GP or to seek a formal assessment from your local child development team.

1. What does your toddler do when you call her name?
   a) She doesn't show any recognition of her name.

b) She seems to respond to her name but she can get very caught up in her own little world.

c) If I call my toddler's name she looks up immediately and smiles.

2. Does your toddler make eye contact?
   a) She rarely makes eye contact.
   b) She does make eye contact with me but will often return to what she's doing.
   c) My toddler looks me in the eye when we chat and often looks around my face, mouth and back at my eyes when I'm talking to her.

3. My toddler is very independent about helping herself in tasks.
   a) My toddler sorts out her own problems but will sometimes drag me to get something if she can't reach.
   b) My toddler is fairly independent but does gesture and ask for help.
   c) My toddler makes frequent verbal and non-verbal requests for help.

4. If you point at something across the room, does your toddler look at it?
   a) It can be quite hard to attract her attention and then she looks at me, not where I'm pointing and can quickly lose interest.
   b) It can be hard to get her attention but she will look if I get in her eyeline, make it very obvious what I'm pointing at, and am very enthusiastic.
   c) Yes, she's always enthusiastic when I show her things and responds to my pointing with a smile or a clap of the hands.

5. Can your toddler hear sounds other than voices?
   a) My toddler turns quickly and startles at loud noises and generally looks in the direction of a new noise such as the phone ringing.

b) She sometimes doesn't hear, especially in the winter months when she's all congested.

c) I sometimes worry that she doesn't respond to quite loud noises.

6. Does your toddler take part in pretend play?
   a) All her friends will play pretend or pretend items are other things and she doesn't at all.
   b) It's hard to tell as she generally uses toys for the purpose.
   c) She uses a wooden block to be a train or a mobile phone, for example, and if I blow on pretend food and say it's hot, she will copy and do it too.

7. Does your toddler have any unusual repetitive habits?
   a) She has an array of noises, hand-flapping and repetitive movements that she spends time doing.
   b) She sometimes runs up and down the room or round in a circle in her own world.
   c) Not really.

8. Does your toddler show you things or what she's doing?
   a) If she's enjoying something she is totally engrossed and doesn't show me or look at me when I ask her what she's playing with.
   b) She can get really into her toys but I can usually get her attention and ask her to show me what she's playing with.
   c) My toddler will often use her play with toys as a way to share an interaction. She will offer me the toy or ask me to help her with words or gestures. It's generally a shared experience.

9. How does your toddler react to being tickled?
   a) She laughs but doesn't make eye contact or share the experience.
   b) She anticipates the tickle and laughs.
   c) She loves tickling games and squeals with delight at the anticipation with full eye contact throughout.

10. Does your toddler like to line up her toys?
    a) She lines up lots of things like wooden blocks, cars, little figures and seems to prefer doing this than playing with them.
    b) She sometimes sorts things into colours or lines up her number cards as she loves numbers and letters.
    c) She never really lines up her toys unless it's part of an imagination game.

Mostly As: Your toddler is displaying many of the behaviours that other parents have reported in their children that have gone on to be diagnosed with autism spectrum disorders. Early diagnosis can hugely support social development and communication skills so it's worth speaking to your GP if you feel your toddler isn't displaying typical social and communication behaviour for her age.

Mostly Bs: Your toddler displays a mixture of typical development behaviour and some behaviours associated with autism spectrum disorder. If she doesn't respond to her name or look where you point it's worth talking to your GP to see if she should be assessed by the child development team.

Mostly Cs: Your toddler seems to be very sociable and uses every scenario she can to connect socially with people. She asks for help, shares eye contact, and enjoys sharing toys and books for the connection they provide as much for the actual toys and books themselves.

chapter seven

the importance of play

'Man is most nearly himself when he achieves the seriousness of a child at play.'

Heraclitus

All mammal babies learn through play, from kittens pouncing on balls of wool to play-fighting puppies. The more intelligent the species is, the longer the 'childhood' and the more playing they do.

It should come as no surprise then to recognise that humans are perhaps without equal in both our love of play and the length of our childhoods. Every culture and tribe that has been studied confirms that their children play (even if they also work); it is one of the few universals of childhood.

Play is serious business for toddlers and this is where they best learn. There is no need to be forever getting out the flashcards; you just have to encourage your toddler to play and play and play.

One of the fundamental jobs of a parent is to keep their toddler safe from danger and disease. However, in a world of antibacterial sprays and lifestyle magazines it can feel like our toddlers should always look squeaky clean and be able to play on an immaculate cream rug while we upload images of perfection to Instagram and Pinterest. These images of perfection can actually do a disservice to your toddler; it is essential that she is allowed to get messy and enjoy uninhibited play where possible.

Messy and sensory play

Maria Montessori (1870–1915) is one of the most influential early years educators and her methods shape much of nursery education today. Her teaching practices were based on the idea that children use all their senses to learn and they are naturally drawn to the right learning experiences for them. Children also are driven by the process of playing, and not just the end result.

Since the manufacture of mass-produced toys and an increasing insistence on cleanliness and 100 per cent safety, some children miss out on really wonderful messy and sensory play. Even as an adult it can be lovely to walk through mud in bare feet or stroke a velvet cushion. When you think about 'sensory' play it's as simple as thinking about the different senses and how they can be activated, including touch, smell, taste, vision, sound, gravity and balance. These activities boost learning, development and creativity.

Below are lots of ideas to help your toddler learn through her senses. Some of them you can plan for and some of them you should just take advantage of when the moment arises. Toddlers love to live in the moment and take advantage of something exciting. Try not to restrict play to specific play areas and playtime.

- You open a package full of bubble wrap, shredded paper or maize/polystyrene packaging beads. Your toddler will get lots of fun and learning from squashing the bubble wrap and loose packaging with her fingers, hands and stomping feet. You could put very messy packaging in the bath if you prefer, and let her play with you keeping an eye. Don't deny yourself either... what other companion in daily life would let you spend 20 minutes popping bubble wrap?
- You're walking through the park on a warm day and the sprinklers are on. The feeling of the wet grass under her toes and the shock when the sprinkler moves and she is suddenly hit with a wall of rain is invaluable and priceless.

- The same goes for if you come across a massive puddle. I remember walking through the centre of Cambridge where a water pipe had burst in summer. There was a beautiful, clear and deep brook running down the main pedestrian street. My son was entranced and not only splashed away but actually body surfed down the water again and again. I was a bit embarrassed as he was completely soaked but seeing the complete joy on his face as he splashed and surfed in the clear water will stay with me forever. I had to run to the market and get him a dry T-shirt and shorts to change into, but it was worth it.

- Mud is another joyful experience. You need to be careful with some mud; only choose shallow mud to play in (my mum had to be rescued from the muddy banks of her local river as a child by the local farmer with ropes and a tractor!). Let your toddler walk through mud and enjoy the sensation of soft mud oozing through her toes.

MAKE A SENSORY TREASURE BOX

Fill a show box with things that might be interesting such as pebbles (large enough not to put in her mouth), pine cones and shells. Each has its own texture. Add different fabrics too, including fake fur, velvet, velcro and fleece. Find objects that smell interesting such as a fresh lemon and a bunch of lavender. Add interesting objects such as measuring spoons, safe cookie cutters. Change the treasures as you like. Your toddler can enjoy rummaging around in the box and examining anything interesting to her, but always supervise her.

- A lot of your toddler's early experimenting with food and solids is a form of sensory play. She is happy to multitask when she eats and who can blame her. I remember loving to sculpt my mashed potato as much as I enjoyed eating it. A snack of berries, cut-up fruits and broccoli lollipops will be a feast for the eyes, nose and fingers as well as a feast for her tummy. Noodles and cooked spaghetti are wonderful to touch and hold.

- Whether it's bath time or washing up time, toddlers have a natural affinity with water. It's great sensory play and also a great opportunity to learn about the natural laws of physics with the behaviour of liquids. Give her a variety of objects and let her see what objects float and which sink. Try to include some natural objects like sticks, corks, lentils, seeds and stones to test too.

- Cardboard boxes deserve a chapter all of their own. They are endlessly versatile and few toys inside can compete with the possibilities of a cardboard box. One idea is to find a very large packing box and turn it into a tunnel; toddlers love to crawl through.

Finger play with a variety of substances with great textures is great sensory play. You could make finger paints with coloured cornflour and water, make or buy some play dough to shape, squash and cut. Playing with bowls of dried ingredients like lentils, pasta and rice is interesting, though if your toddler keeps putting them in her mouth you may prefer to try this again when she is older. Sand is great for fingers, and a full sand pit with buckets, rakes, funnels and spades is full of play potential. It's fun when it's dry and warm and even better for building when it's damp.

Creative play and toddler art development

There is a fascinating and charming development in the art your child will produce from toddlerhood through to adulthood.

Toddlers begin experimenting with mark-making; whether it be chalks on paving in the garden, finger paints or patterns in the mud. Their ability to make marks is built up of recognisable building blocks. By their second birthday toddlers are usually able to draws rough circles, lines and dots. By 30 months they can make a horizontal line, V-shape, T-shape and a more considered circle. By your toddler's third birthday you will begin to see the classic figure with limbs coming out of the head, and she may also add an H-shape to her repertoire of word shapes. She may also begin to hold a crayon with her thumb, index and middle fingers in the so-called 'dynamic tripod grasp' because of the three digits involved. At first your toddler's drawing is limited by her fine motor skills, but in time her pincer grip will be more controlled.

What is going on in their heads is interesting. As an adult we can hold the concept of an image such as a horse in our head, and then represent it in a drawing. Toddlers can't do this so they draw and then may label the picture *afterwards* (especially when an adult asks them what the drawing is!).

Art development seems to follow recognisable milestones. People are the most popular things to draw. Most toddlers will start by drawing just faces, then the faces have limbs coming out of them until eventually the people have bodies. It is lovely to see your child's drawing develop and really worth using an app or a folder to keep examples of the stages her art goes through.

I love the confidence and unselfconscious way that children create and draw. One of my favourite stories was from a TED talk by Sir Ken Robinson where he talks about creativity in children. He recounted how he was talking to a young four-year-old in a classroom, and asking her what she was drawing. She replied she was drawing a picture of God. Sir Ken said: 'But no one knows what God looks like.' To which the girl charmingly replied: 'They will in a minute!'

Make time for arts, crafts and mark-making with your toddler and try not to guide or correct her creations. For toddlers the end result really isn't the point. They enjoy the flow, the moment and the act of creating.

Drawing development tests

Toddlers and older children seem to master new stages in their ability to draw and write in a similar way. The changes can be quite subtle so if you are interested in how your toddler's skills and abilities are being refined you might like to:

- notice when your toddler draws a vertical line
- notice when your toddler draws a horizontal line
- ask your toddler to draw a circle (or copy a circle that you have drawn)
- ask your toddler to draw a cross
- ask your toddler to draw a person
- ask your toddler to draw something they could have never seen before, e.g. a bicycle with triangle wheels or a man with two heads.

Social play and pretend play

Seeing your toddler hosting a pretend tea party with you and her teddy bears is a really lovely milestone in your toddler's development. Pretend play is where a child will use representative items to play and enact real interactions, so when your toddler holds a brick to her ear and pretends to talk on the phone this is a real cognitive leap.

The next leap in play is when your toddler is able to play with another child and share pretend play. This generally requires more language, although my autistic nephew was able to have pretend tea parties with his cousins before he was able to speak. In pretend play two children are improvising and they need to explain what their props are and what they are doing. Obviously this becomes much easier when a child can hold up a banana and say 'ring' 'ring', 'Mummy on phone'. Adults will fill in the blanks and suggest story lines but toddlers find this hard to do so initial shared play is basic in plot but rich in connection.

Play in all its forms is how your toddler's brain understands the world. During play your toddler will be effortlessly testing her hypotheses about the world and the items in her environment. So whilst it all looks very disorganised and simple, play is the way your toddler's brain systematically learns how the world works.

real parent story

Jon (Tilly, 26 months)

'Cats and toddlers are obsessed with cardboard boxes. If I get something delivered in a big box it's such a bonus as I know both Tilly and the cats will be messing around in it for ages. I know it's a cliché but Tilly usually prefers the box that the toy came in than the toy itself, so I now try and repurpose boxes for her to play with as it's cheaper and greener and she loves to play with real things.'

Quiz: Play and learning preferences

All children learn by seeing, hearing and moving. However, you may begin to see slight preferences emerge in what kind of play and learning your toddler is drawn to. Try to encourage lots of different ways of interacting with toys and the environment.

1. If you take your toddler to a playgroup, does she choose:
   a) Making lots of pictures and paintings at the painting table.
   b) To make lots of noise with the musical instruments.
   c) Climbing frame and ball even when inside.

2. If you need to keep your toddler occupied before a doctor's appointment do you:
   a) Give her a crayon and paper.
   b) Let her listen to a song on your headphones.
   c) Play 'ladies horses' or another song where you jog your toddler up and down on your knee.

3. My toddler loves:
   a) Sharing picture books.
   b) Loud toys that make noises.
   c) Anything that lets her move and climb.

4. When you share a book with your toddler is she:
   a) Still and entranced by the images, often going back a page to look at a picture.
   b) Happy to listen to rhythmic stories and looks up and watches you reading.
   c) Very fidgety and prefers interactive books like *We're going on a bear hunt.*

5. If your toddler sees your smartphone does she prefer:
   a) Watching videos and looking at the photos you've taken.
   b) Listening to your songs.
   c) Playing a game.

Mostly As: Visual learner
Your toddler may remember the pictures in books and love painting with colours. As she gets older she may find pictures and shapes help her to learn new concepts, e.g. photos of real apples added to real oranges to help with counting.

Mostly Bs: Auditory learner
Some children process information most effectively if they can hear it, such as verbal instructions and rhymes. Your toddler will love stories and will be happy to lie in the dark and listen to a story more so than other children. When your child gets older she may love to listen to podcasts and audiobooks rather than read.

Mostly Cs: Kinetic learner
All toddlers learn when they are physically immersed in an activity. Your toddler may go on to be very physically confident and get fidgety if she has to sit still for a period of time. She will probably find physical skills like tying shoelaces easy and may even understand concepts physically, for example, playing with old-fashioned scales to feel the weights as they are placed in each pan.

TOP TIP

Toddlers are world experts at play and do not need you to buy them tonnes of plastic toys. Items you have around the home, or discover when out and about can be as, if not more, exciting.

part two
classic toddler challenges

'The fundamental job of a toddler is to rule the universe.'
Lawrence Kutner

In this part of the book you will learn about why parents encounter classic flashpoints with their toddlers. Although each toddler is an individual, they are all travelling through the same developmental milestones which produce flashpoints that, as a parent, you need to manage.

These flashpoints include the 'terrible two' classics, including tantrums, inability to delay gratification, biting and reluctance to share. Every parent of a toddler will recognise these challenges that can cause lots of frustration, anger and upset to both toddlers and parents. Once you understand how your toddler's mind works you will be able to empathise with him better and learn to manage his behaviour at each flashpoint.

chapter eight

no! emerging
independence

'Nothing is more precious than independence and liberty.'
Ho Chi Minh

The path to independence is uniquely slow in human beings. It's a long process, not a one-off event – ask any parent of a college student! As animals go, we have the longest childhood of any species. Childhood is the time we get most learning and support from our parents and families and toddlerhood is the first time that our children become mobile and motivated to exert choice. Toddlers become much less passive and show strong (and often repetitive) preferences for certain things.

When you have a toddler and first hear that emphatic 'no!' it should be celebrated and respected. Saying 'no' is an indication of your toddler taking a huge jump in thinking. Instead of a passive acceptance of her environment she is beginning to discriminate between things she likes and things she doesn't like. She is also beginning to realise that her needs and preferences do not completely overlap with yours. Asserting her choice is vital. This doesn't mean giving in to every demand, but don't see this as a continual battle of wills where all opposition must be quashed to avoid raising a brat. Your child does need to have some of his own opinions in life! So many parents exhaust themselves and their toddlers by making huge battles out of everything. Choosing your battles will need to be a central pillar of your parenting style with your toddler. The dangers of battling with your toddler and crushing their will over **everything** include:

- your toddler is incapable of absorbing a logical argument when upset
- battles deregulate your toddler's emotions further and he can lose control
- squashing your toddler's opinion can be bullying and doesn't broaden his understanding
- battles are upsetting and tiring for both of you
- constant battles can create unnecessary adversarial patterns
- your toddler may withdraw if you battle with him
- your toddler may amplify his behaviour and become more aggressive if you battle with him.

Try to remember that your toddler needs your help to regulate his emotions and help him understand the rules and boundaries in a way that makes him feel that you are on his side not in opposition. This is particularly important as he will need to feel that you are his secure base of unconditional love as he feels his way and develops greater independence.

Separation and independence develop in recognised stages from birth. Newborn babies do not even 'know' that you are not a part of them. From around six months, babies begin to realise that their parents are separate from them and can leave them alone. This can lead to separation anxiety, when previously relaxed babies can become very clingy and frightened every time their parents leave the room. Separation anxiety is still very powerful in toddlers too.

If your toddler has separation anxiety or is 'clingy', it is important to respect his fear and help him to develop coping skills so that he learns that you always come back and that he can cope and be happy without you. This means saying goodbye when you need to leave for a period of time, explaining you are coming back, providing comfort objects (see page 189), and, of course, leaving him with someone who cares and acts as his secure base in your absence.

Your exploring toddler

One aspect of independence that is very characteristic of toddlers is wanting things their own way. Toddlers have strong impulses to explore and will often respond with anger and aggression if they are incapable of, or prevented from doing what they want.

Toddlers are innately curious about the world around them and as soon as they are mobile they will seek out new experiences. This is an important process, taking them from helpless infant to learning child to independent adult. However, it can be very hard work for you as a parent, as toddlers are working to their own agenda (exploring the planet) and their own timetable (now!) and do not care about your plans. We are all very familiar with toddlers who are becoming increasingly independent. They want to do things themselves, they want to choose where they go and what they do, and they are very loud and vocal about it! Toddlers soon learn to say 'no' and 'me do it'.

Toddlers are not yet able to empathise with another person's needs (see page 151) so can seem very single-minded and focused on their own agenda. This means they will run off to explore, or stay behind to investigate, or get angry if they are unable to explore. This is compounded by the fact that toddlers can't yet express themselves fully and so become easily frustrated when you don't understand what they want to do.

Imagine if you had just arrived on a new planet and kept being frustrated in your attempts to explore – it would be infuriating. This is how toddlers feel when you insist they ignore all the fascinating things around them and go with you quickly to do something they are not interested in. All children should be encouraged to develop their independence at a comfortable pace and you will need to build in time to accommodate this. There will be several flashpoints when you need to accommodate your toddler's independence:

- travelling from A to B. Toddlers tend to see the journey as important as the destination so you will need to leave earlier than if you were travelling by yourself
- learning a new skill. Toddlers will become less happy to be passive in their care. This emerging desire for self-care needs to be encouraged, which admittedly takes a lot of patience (as you will appreciate if you've ever been running late while your toddler insists on putting on his own socks or gloves!)
- encountering a novel item. You may have seen hundreds of dishwashers, dogs and dandelion clocks, but your toddler will notice all the new things around him and will be strongly driven to investigate them
- time management. Toddlers run to a very different clock to adults. Sometimes their clock is running at high speed as their attention flits from one thing to the next and they can't seem to stay still and slow with you. At other times their clock is running at slow speed. In these moments your toddler is 'in the zone' with something and experiencing 'flow' – he is utterly engrossed and time stands still for him – and for you!

I am not suggesting that your toddler's agenda should run everything. Rather, that by understanding the reality of how your toddler's emerging independence will play out during the day you can manage your own schedule and expectations, as well as your toddler's.

Intrepid versus cautious explorers

Not all toddlers are the same. For every thrill-seeking toddler there will be a toddler who is more cautious and finds new people and experiences stressful. This so called 'behavioural inhibition' (see page 19) seems to be quite hard-wired, and it is important to respond to your toddler's individual needs. Shy, cautious toddlers will need lots of encouragement and to see his parents:

- picking up worms and bugs
- getting dirty
- jumping off things
- meeting new people
- getting stuck into new activities with confidence and pleasure.

On the other hand, some toddlers are so bold and impulsive that they will need more messages about being safe and slowing down. If you have a bold and independent toddler it is a good idea to take him to big spaces so that you can safely supervise him without micro-managing and stultifying his play. Soft play centres can be great as the areas have been designed to promote exploration and physical activity without the need for you to helicopter around them. When you are out and about it can help to choose locations where you have a long line of sight so that you can give your toddler a free rein. Examples of the places I took my toddler when they were being intrepid include:

- big beaches at low tide, e.g. Holkham Beach in Norfolk
- empty tennis courts in the morning
- empty skate parks before the teenagers get up and descend on the place
- empty shopping centre malls as they just open
- big open commons with 'nowhere to hide'.

Your role is to be your toddler's secure base from which he explores the world. It seems counter-intuitive, but children who have the securest bonds with their parents are more likely to become independent, resilient and confident. As a parent this means being consistent, loving your child, and spending time interacting with them.

Choose a safe environment

Toddlers should be allowed to try, fail and improve at lots of new skills from balancing on a log to putting on socks. However, toddlers are not able to assess the risks they encounter when out and about. We all know which environments require close supervision by an adult so choose locations that don't have dangerous traffic, large drops, deep water, etc. before you give your child freedom to explore safely. Make sure the environment provides lots of opportunities to take safe risks: balancing on stepping stones, jumping in puddles, picking up creepy crawlies.

However, toddlers also need to slowly learn to be safe in their environment. This means teaching your toddler rules which are non-negotiable. If you choose your battles it makes it easier to have your list of non-negotiable boundaries. These rules might include:

- if you are walking down a busy road your toddler needs to hold your hand or go in the pushchair
- he has to wear the belt or harness in the car, pushchair and highchair
- all toddlers need to learn that 'stop!' means stop. You can play games to help him learn the concept. Practise him freezing when you say 'stop!' or 'freeze!' I also taught my toddlers to stop at road edges and bollards.

Sometimes let your child do the daft thing. If he wants to try biting a lemon, let him; it is how he will learn. Let him have lots of different, but safe, experiences. Children who constantly hear 'be careful, be careful' are more likely to be anxious.

Stubbornness

With a burgeoning independence can come an almost comical stubbornness in your toddler.

This self-destructive stubbornness is familiar to all parents of toddlers. Whether your toddler is adamant he doesn't want a coat in the snow, insists that he wants to taste the vindaloo curry, or wears his best shoes out in the rain, it seems at these moments all 'social referencing' of their parents' behaviour and advice goes out the window. (See page 172.)

I think every parent of a toddler has had a moment where they have encountered that steely determination, stubbornness and impulsivity to take control only to choose something inappropriate. I think a sense of humour is vital here, because toddlers are loveable and ludicrous in equal measure. You have to be in awe of their chutzpah and joie de vivre, but at the same time help them as they learn about cause and effect.

TOP TIP

If your toddler insists on having a lemon for pudding it's fine to let them learn the sour lesson that your suggestion would have been more delicious. Obviously, if the choice is dangerous or hurts someone else, you wouldn't indulge it, but try to be charmed rather than exasperated by your toddler's tenacity.

Toddler travel: getting your toddler from A to B

Adults are very future-focused and our brains can accommodate delaying gratification by sitting in a car for a long journey to go on holiday or walking in the rain to get to a party. Your toddler could not be more different. He really lives in the moment, so during a journey, the journey is the thing. The best way to help your toddler get from A to B with minimum fuss, and hopefully a bit of joy, is to get down to his level, live in the moment, and enjoy the journey. This means that however you are travelling – by foot, by car or by plane – you need to be prepared with games and activities to play with your toddler.

Enjoy the micro-cosmos

If you are planning to walk somewhere with your toddler you need to build in lots of time 'for the journey'. Your toddler fundamentally understands that the journey is just as important as the destination and will notice and absorb everything. This is because he is not thinking about the future, about playgroup, or whatever it is that awaits. He is smelling the flowers and spotting the ladybirds. Many adults would benefit from this approach to life too, and you will really lower your stress levels and arrive with a much happier and enriched toddler if you slow down to his pace and 'take the time to smell the roses'. You can even pack a bucket or a mini magnifying glass so the walk becomes a micro safari. This really is both a precious learning and bonding time, so set off early so you don't need to rush.

INVISIBLE JOURNEYS

One of the best ways to get your toddler from A to B, especially if he is tired and dragging his feet, is to make him travel without realising he's travelling by starting a moving game to distract him.

I play jumping over the shadows of bikes as they whizz past us with my youngest on the way to and back from school. She can be transformed from a whinger with the energy of a 100 year old, to a bounding show-jumping pony. Before she knows it we are nearly home and she is now in a good mood! There are lots of variants on this game, such as jumping over cracks in the pavement or puddles, but the ploy is the same. You are distracting your toddler from focusing on the walk and changing his focus onto a moving game.

Trapped toddlers

If you are both stuck waiting in a café or a doctor's surgery, make-believe games are a fantastic way to keep your older toddler happy. Ask your toddler what kind of cupcake he wants you to make him in your cupcake shop. You can describe the cupcake in all its amazing detail, from rainbow icing to fairy dust sprinkles, and you can even mime making it, icing it and taking payment from him. Then it's his turn.

I feel really sorry for toddlers held fast in car seats on a long journey. Can you imagine having to wear a five-point harness for hours in a car? Again, his world in the car is very boring and unchanging so he needs distracting. Games like 'I Spy' are perfect, though to play it with young toddlers you will need to be descriptive, rather than use letters: 'I spy with my little eye, something that I like to drink in the car' etc. If your toddler loves lorries, get him to shout out 'lorry' every time you pass one on the motorway. If your toddler's language isn't up to verbal games yet, you can ask him, for example, 'Can you see the big green lorry, point at the green lorry!' This allows time to pass, and with naps and frequent stops your toddler will be much happier on a long car trip.

Some toddlers like a sing-along. My daughter would love us to sing 'Hey Diddle Diddle' but only joined in the word at the end of each line when she was just learning to sing. You can either sing a cappella or take a CD or playlist of nursery rhymes for the car.

If they prefer to use their hands you could put some tactile toys or there are even little steering wheels that you can attach in front of them if they want to drive like you!

real parent story

Gillian (Louis, 3 years)

'If I could have my time again with Louis I would not have so many face-offs with him. I didn't want him to become spoilt so I would spend my time saying 'don't do this' and 'don't do that' – he had lots of tantrums and I was so tired of the constant disciplining. It was upsetting and wasted a lot of energy. If I have another one I will lighten up!'

TOP TIP

Choose your battles. Your toddler does need boundaries but crushing him every time he wants to do something or says 'no' will escalate battles like an arms race. Side-tracking (see page 00) your toddler can often help to defuse face-offs.

grr! aggression

'Man must evolve for all human conflict a method which rejects revenge, aggression and retaliation. The foundation of such a method is love.'

Martin Luther King, Jr

Toddlerhood provides the perfect storm for aggression, and it is a universal trait in toddlers. Toddlers are impulsive and single-minded; when your toddler is thwarted by other people she is unable to put herself in the shoes of the person who has got in her way. Put two toddlers together who both:

- lack impulse control
- can't articulate their desires with language
- find it impossible to put themselves in the shoes of others
- want their own way

and aggression is inevitable.

However, there is a wide range in the aggression displayed by different toddlers. Psychologists rate behaviour on a spectrum from aggressive, externalising or acting out, to non-aggressive, internalising and withdrawn. Basically, when we feel strong emotions inside, this spectrum helps to describe what can be seen from the outside. Aggressive toddlers wear their emotions on their sleeves and do not hold back what they are feeling.

Biting

It is so upsetting, not to mention embarrassing, if your toddler bites another child. It's such a painful form of aggression that it's very hard for the victim's parents to be relaxed about it.

Toddlers tend to resort to biting when they feel overwhelmed and frustrated by other children. (Toddlers may also bite for other reasons, such as to experiment, or sometimes if they are teething.) The reassuring fact is that biting is quite common and isn't evidence that your toddler is going to be a violent and aggressive child.

Toddlers have strong impulses but are too young to explain, negotiate or empathise with their playmates. This means that they find sharing or turn-taking really difficult. One of the gentlest toddlers I have ever known had a biting phase and it was such a stressful time for his mum. I wasn't at all surprised that he stopped biting quite quickly when she implemented the advice I outline here. He grew up to become an empathic and calm little boy.

If your toddler enters a biting phase try not to avoid groups and play dates as a result. Rather than hide away your toddler, try to make sure that you are ready to step in when you see things escalating to a biting incident. I'm afraid this will mean several sessions where you will need to be on hand to manage your toddler to make sure that no other toddler gets bitten. As with many things prevention is better. If your toddler is supervised it gives her lots of opportunity to learn to take turns and that other children have feelings too.

How can I prevent my toddler from biting?

As the world expert on your own toddler you will see the flashpoints, the factors that lead to her losing control. Tired, frustrated, stressed and hungry toddlers are more likely to lash out. This is the same for all people; you know yourself that if you are running late or have low blood sugar, for example, you may be grumpy and lash out (verbally at least ... although adults banging their hands on computers and stuck freezer drawers is not unheard of).

A large part of looking after your toddler is managing and avoiding your toddler being overtired, thirsty or hungry. These basics come before play dates or classes as your toddler is just not receptive to anything if she doesn't feel warm, rested and comfortable.

Apart from managing these basic needs you need to read how your toddler is reacting to situations. If you are unable to prevent factors that make things worse (e.g. hunger), you can teach your toddler to give you a signal when she reaches a flash-point. I read of one mum who taught her biting toddler to sign 'help' (with a simple hand in the air – like when you want to get a teacher's attention) when he wasn't coping, and the mum was then able to step in and help before things got to a biting incident.

What should I do if my toddler bites another child?

If your toddler does bite say 'no' in a calm but authoritative tone. Remove your toddler from the vicinity of the child and go to the victim. Tell the victim that you are sorry and that you know it hurts to be bitten. You may also need to perform first aid or seek medical help if the bite is very bad or on the face.

Looking after the victim is important as they are the injured party, and it also shows in strong terms to your toddler that she doesn't get attention when she bites – she will see that you respond to the victim and not her.

When the victim is being looked after by their own parent or carer, you can go to your child. She will probably be very upset but you need to check the victim is okay and being looked after before you can see to your toddler. This is not a moment to be 'seen to parent' (there are actually no moments where you should think about your public perfor-mance). The most effective way you can teach your toddler that biting is not okay is to quietly, firmly and calmly explain that biting is bad as it hurts people. No more, no less. Lots of explanation will dilute the message and if your toddler is upset she will not be in a receptive mode. This isn't bad behaviour, this is 'emotional deregulation' or, put simply, she has lost the plot and needs to be calmed down before she can listen to you.

To help your toddler to come out of her biting phase quickly it is important to agree a consistent plan with your partner, grandparents, nursery staff and other carers so that you are all working together. It really won't help if one person decides to try their own technique and please don't let adults bite your toddler back. This is because the message your toddler will take from this is not just 'an eye for an eye', but that physical aggression is okay if the aggressor is a big adult.

It's important that together you are consistent in:

- learning to see the warning signs of a biting incident
- teaching your toddler to have a signal if she is getting frustrated to ask for your help
- giving a firm, authoritative 'no' if she tries to bite (intervene and stop this happening)
- give a consistent message that biting is bad and biting hurts
- read stories about biting, e.g. *Teeth are Not for Biting* by Elizabeth Verdick.

Try to remember that biting is a common (though aggressive and unpleasant) behaviour and that your toddler will grow out of it with your help. With a consistent approach your toddler will learn to cope with frustration and other children's needs in a more acceptable way. Hopefully, before too long it will all be a distant memory.

Shouting, kicking and other forms of aggression

There are many ways that toddlers can be aggressive, from roaring and screaming, to pulling hair, hitting, kicking and throwing objects. You take the same approach as with biting (see page 131):

- first, intervene and stop the aggression
- second, check the victim of your toddler's aggression is okay
- third, take your toddler to one side and calm her down with a quiet and soothing presence
- fourth, simply explain that we don't, e.g. pull hair as it hurts.

If your toddler is hurting herself or smashing up the place you need to calm her down in the first instance. She has lost control, she can't hear or process your 'important life lessons' until you help her to calm down first. In the long term you need to identify what is winding up your toddler and if there is a pattern. You also need to reduce the factors that make aggression worse namely hunger, fatigue, cold, overheating, noise, even strong smells. These internal and external factors make everyone feel tetchy; for a toddler it can mean a full-on aggressive meltdown.

Playing nicely

Toddler playgroups are invaluable opportunities for playing and interaction. It's a fine line between supervising parents and adults managing breakdowns in interaction, and micromanaging every moment of play.

Toddlers can experience a multitude of emotions and experiences in just a few minutes. They will learn lots of important lessons from adults helping them to play 'nicely' and they will learn just as much from the often wordless (but frequently vocal) interactions. Toddlers model behaviour so it can help to play with them, but also to let them play with older cousins and siblings so that they model good standards of behaviour towards others. It can be frustrating if your toddler picks up a 'bad habit' or shares a bad behaviour with another child. If you feel that your toddler is modelling some bad behaviour you can try and mix up their play a bit so they get to share time with a range of other children. Don't feel that you have to be completely passive about who your toddler plays with. That's not to say that you need to ostracise other toddlers, but just try to make sure that she has the opportunity to play with toddlers who display lots of gentle, empathic and good-humoured behaviour as they can be great teachers for your toddler.

When I took my toddlers along to playgroups it often struck me that it was a little like having your own 'eccentric' friend along; that you had to apologise for, intercede on behalf of, and protect. All the parents are in the same boat, although some parents had a tougher time depending on the idiosyncrasies of their toddler. At a nice, welcoming playgroup this is well understood and there is a sense of camaraderie. If you feel that the playgroup that you and your toddler attend is becoming too stressful it might be worth meeting up in a smaller group with a couple of like-minded parents to go to the park, or try out a few playgroups until you find one that both you and your toddler enjoy.

At any playgroup, bullying and aggression should be stopped. In a large room full of exciting toys and excited toddlers it's not really an option to get lost in a magazine or your phone and hope for the best. That day will come, but toddlers need help in these early days of socialising. Again, this does not mean micro-managing every interaction; a few pushes, grunts and hard stares are part of toddler life and help your toddler to realise that other children want to play with the same toys as them and that turn-taking helps to make things fair for everybody.

Learning to share

There are opportunities to learn about sharing and turn-taking every day with toddlers:

- if you are making a snack for your toddler and a friend make sure that your toddler helps get the snack and gives the snack to the friend

- give your toddler lots of opportunities to help you share food out at mealtimes, e.g. one tomato for you and one for me
- if you are playing with sets of toys share them out, e.g. you can have ten bricks and your friend can have ten bricks
- at the park police the swing and the slide with your toddler and her friends, e.g. your friend can have 20 pushes then it's your turn for 20 pushes. Keep the turns short so that your toddler doesn't have to delay gratification for too long and it will become a habit for her.

---

real parent story

Jenny (Robert, 3½ years)

'Robert went through a horrible phase of pinching faces. It was always other toddlers at the local church coffee morning as there were lots of toys, and if anyone tried to take his toy or use it too he'd push or pinch their face hard. Luckily I had quite a few friends there that knew neither of us was a maniac but for a while I was always hovering near him and had lots of cold lattes. By the time he was three he just got better at sharing and not getting so angry. Practice makes perfect I suppose.'

Quiz: Does your behaviour affect your toddler's aggression?

All toddlers will be aggressive, physically hurt other people and damage things at one time or another. However, your attitudes around aggression and your own aggression can be a model to your toddler. Some behaviours can promote aggression in your toddler, and some behaviours can promote emotional regulation and alternatives to aggression. This quiz will help you think about how you respond to your toddler's behaviour.

1. If your toddler hits another toddler at a playgroup do you:
   a) Have your nose buried in a magazine when you go to playgroup, it's a little bit of me-time.

b) Try not to interfere too much as they need to slug it out a little bit.

c) Tell her immediately that hitting is not allowed.

2. Do you have consistent rules in your home about aggression such as hitting, kicking and shoving?
   a) I don't really know what to do when my toddler is violent.
   b) Mostly, but if she's tired I let things slide.
   c) Yes, we have the home rules that I am firm about – they are non-negotiatble.

3. Have you suggested ideas for what to do when your toddler feels frustrated and angry?
   a) She can't speak properly yet so it's not something I have discussed with her.
   b) I have told her when I am angry I hit a pillow instead of a person.
   c) I have encouraged her to sign to me when she's losing control and I will help her calm down.

4. Are you pleased when your toddler stands up to other children?
   a) Yes, it's Lord of the Flies out there and she needs to stand her ground.
   b) I think it's important to stick up for yourself but not sure what to suggest to her.
   c) I like my toddler to be assertive and feel confident to say 'no' or whatever but not to lose control and physically hurt another child.

5. What do you do if your toddler hurts you?
   a) Hurt her back.
   b) I make a big deal out of it.
   c) I pull a sad face and explain simply that her shove hurt me.

6. Have you ever smacked your toddler?
   a) I smack my toddler when she's naughty; it's the only language she understands.

b) I have smacked her a few times when I'm at the end of my tether.

c) I have never smacked my toddler.

7. Do you have a temper?

a) I lose my temper quite frequently and find it hard to wind down.

b) I only lose my temper very occasionally and usually calm down quickly.

c) I can't remember losing my temper and when I do it's usually in response to pain and directed at an inanimate object like a piece of Lego I've trodden on!

8. What about conflicts between you and your partner?

a) We have frequent loud rows and blows have been exchanged in front of my toddler.

b) No physical aggression but loud arguments do occur.

c) We have our conflicts but we try and discuss our issues respectfully and resolve them quickly.

9. What do you do when your toddler plays the peacemaker?

a) Heave a sigh of relief that I don't have to weigh in.

b) Say 'well done'.

c) Describe what she did: 'you were very calm when your friend knocked you over by mistake', and give her a hug and say I'm proud of her.

10. Do you make your toddler say sorry?

a) Yes, if she's in the wrong I insist on a sorry or she knows she will be punished.

b) Sometimes, if I am being watched by judgemental parents.

c) No, I explain that it makes a person feel better if you apologise but don't insist.

11. What do you say when your toddler is angry?

a) I tell her she's silly to get angry over such a little thing.

b) I say 'calm down'.

c) I try and acknowledge her anger, however ludicrous it might seem to me as an adult, e.g., 'I know you are very angry that you can't wear your swimsuit in the snow but you will get too cold.'

Mostly As: You behaviour tends to increase the chances that your toddler will act aggressively and your response to their aggression doesn't help her to calm down.

Mostly Bs: You are not very aggressive yourself, but you don't really know how to handle aggression in your toddler and other people in your life.

Mostly Cs: You are very good at regulating your toddler's emotions and help her find alternatives to lashing out and getting angry.

As you will see from the quiz above your behaviour can be subtle but have a profound effect on your toddler's aggression. For example, insisting on an apology is quite a disempowering thing to do and in my experience it is better to explain that **saying** sorry really helps someone who is sad or hurt to feel better.

Body language also an important tool to help her calm down so she can listen to you. Like with a skittish horse or an angry cat, soothing and calming noises and body language help to reduce aggression in people too – every parent can learn to be a toddler whisperer. When your toddler is having a tantrum she's not on 'receiver' mode so you need to calm her and get her attention if you want to impart any life lessons.

TOP TIP

Prevention is best with any aggressive behaviour. You need to anticipate the flashpoints and help your toddler and her friends to work out how to play and share. If incidents happen, remain calm and firm, and quickly show your disapproval.

chapter ten

waa! fears and anxieties

'We cannot always build the future for our youth, but we can build our youth for the future.'

Franklin D. Roosevelt

Fears and anxiety are part and parcel of the toddler years. Your toddler is learning so much about the world, trying to assess risk, and his imagination is beginning to allow him to imagine monsters and scary things. The good news is that you can make a big difference to the way your toddler handles his fears and anxieties. There are some common culprits that cause fear in toddlers across the land. These can include so many things, from fear of the dark to men with beards (including Father Christmas) – there's a lot for toddlers to cope with! As you will see later in the chapter there seems to be a pattern to when some of the fears emerge, and when they recede as your toddler develops.

The function of fear

Fear and anxiety are found throughout the animal kingdom and serve as a survival instinct. If you meet a lion you need the instinct to feel extreme fear and want to escape.

We still retain some of these very ancient fears, such as a fear of snakes. Most toddlers in the UK haven't seen a snake in the wild but if something slithers towards your toddler he will instinctively jump away. It is even observed in people with a damaged visual cortex. So how can it be that a 'blind' person and a toddler who has never seen a snake have this powerful aversion to an unknown reptile? It seems that it was incredibly important in our evolutionary past in Africa to flee quickly from snakes as one bite could kill a child, so there is a direct neural pathway (bypassing the visual cortex) from the optic nerve to the amygdala in the brain. When anticipating danger, the human amygdala quickly boots up the 'flight or fight' response so our heart can start beating faster immediately to pump oxygen to our body so we can get away before the snake strikes.

DID YOU KNOW?

Many phobias that people suffer with come from these ancestral survival imperatives. A person safely inside a skyscraper may have a feeling of fear of the height even though he cannot be harmed.

Childhood fears are usually short-lived, predictable and when they occur don't last forever; for example, a fear of monsters under the bed. My daughter is going through a monster fear at the minute. The monster is called 'Bugus Mugus' and she needs escorting to go and get her socks from the cupboard before school most mornings. Often very imaginative children suffer most with these fears as their imagination is strong and they are able to paint vivid and frightening scenarios in their minds.

Your toddler may know that the monsters aren't real, but their brain has already alerted the amygdala and their hearts still beat faster.

Phobias

Phobias are one kind of anxiety disorder, with a very deep fear that can take over a toddler's life. However, the good news is that you can get rid of them. My son developed a phobia of dogs when he was jumped on and pinned to the ground by a dog as a toddler.

We were able to move him slowly from extreme fear, to moderate fear, to ambivalence, to positive interest by a programme of gradually increasing exposure. We first took him to see our neighbour's dog Milligan while Milligan slept on the ground. On the next visit he stroked Milligan's back as he sat in my lap, then he stroked Milligan's head ('the danger end'). The next step was to go on a walk with Milligan being kept on the lead with me holding the lead. My son soon wanted to hold the lead himself, and finally Milligan was off the lead and running round us and the phobia had gone! Some phobias are quite specific and unusual, e.g. fear of buttons or clowns. I would really recommend, where possible, using similar steps to help your toddler to overcome these fears, especially if your toddler curtails their activities to avoid the subject of their phobia.

How fears and anxieties track your toddler's development

There seems to be a rough timetable of common fears and anxieties which map the age and stage that your child is at. These fears reflect the new dangers he faces, for example, when he becomes mobile.

Before your toddler is truly mobile his main fears will be:

- abandonment or separation (as he cannot follow you)
- strangers
- loud noises or sudden movements (as it's hard for him to flee).

As your toddler's brain develops and is able to hold thoughts, ideas and concepts in his head a new raft of fears develops including:

- night-time darkness and noises
- monsters

- costumes and masks (he is not yet able to understand that a friendly person is behind them)
- beards – this helps explain the montages of toddlers sobbing sitting on Father Christmas' knee on *You've Been Framed*.
- dogs, goats, horses, chickens and ducks (your toddler is slower – and often smaller – than these animals)
- insects and spiders (especially stinging insects that bother him).

How to cope with your toddler's fears

The more you can be a calm, consistent and sensitive parent as your toddler encounters these potentially frightening things the better. If you see that he is frightened, get down to his level, provide lots of touch, cuddles and eye contact, and always be willing to encounter the stimulus first to show him it's okay, e.g. holding a worm or stroking a friendly dog.

As your toddler gets older and his environment expands he will continually face new fears and anxieties, whether at day care or on a day trip. You will need to anticipate and guide him to help him cope with new and unknown fears by reassuring him that he always has someone to go to if he is frightened and that you always make sure that he isn't in danger.

Whether these fears are the result of real experiences or imagined, your toddler is not able to regulate his emotions and calm himself down so he does need your help. Try not to belittle his fears, e.g., 'Don't be silly, it's only a dog!' or 'Monsters don't exist – so please just go upstairs and don't turn the light on.' He needs more help than that.

If your child is scared of his wardrobe, you need to break down the components of his fear – he doesn't like the dark, being alone, the possibility of monsters. You can remove these aspects of the fear and reintroduce them when he has overcome the fear. So start with the lights on and you there. Then try you being down the hall while he is there with the light on etc.

One great weapon against fear is laughter. When my children were scared of a person I always told them to imagine them sat on the loo having a poo! I know it's not very mature, but it has helped my children ever since they developed 'toilet humour'. If your toddler's language isn't so developed, you could say 'silly monster with silly purple head' or similar in a cavalier fashion; it can help him to reframe the monster in his mind as unthreatening.

In my PhD I developed a 'scary situation task' which involved asking the parent to ask their child to reach into a large black box and retrieve rubber insects. The 'low anxiety' parents used similar techniques to help their child's fear evaporate. Here are my tips based on this experiment:

1. always offer to take on the scary thing first
2. act as your toddler's human shield
3. never ask him to do what you are afraid to do yourself – especially if you are displaying fear at the time
4. don't just deny that your toddler is afraid
5. be calm and confident. *How* you talk to your toddler when he is scared is more important than *what* you say.

When helping your toddler to deal with a fear, work out his 'comfort zone'. Don't force way beyond it, but don't let your toddler completely avoid his fears all the time. Make slow steps to gently cope with his fears, such as: 'How about if I stroke the dog while you sit on my lap?'

Anxiety, fears and temperament

Toddlers come with different temperaments and you may find that your toddler is naturally more fearful and anxious than some others. Some toddlers are bold, while some are more timid and shy. Harvard developmental psychologist, Jerome Kagan, has found these differences in babies as young as three months old and often these temperamental differences between babies are fairly stable and persist. This dimension of temperament is called 'behavioural inhibition'. Differences in behavioural inhibition seem to be largely down to the sensitivity of an individual's amygdala. The amygdala is in the ancient 'reptile' part of the brain and deals with immediate danger. If your senses perceive danger, such as a predator, the amygdala will light up and your 'fight or flight' response will kick in. Studies of toddlers with high behavioural inhibition (and who are therefore more reserved and shy) found their amygdala was significantly more sensitive compared with their bolder counterparts who display low behavioural inhibition.

Kagan tested children's behavioural inhibition with a range of stimuli, such as bright flashing robots and strangers. Toddlers who are timid and fearful of the stimuli at a young age seem to remain so even when tested several years later. The same was generally true for the bold infants – when they returned to the lab years later they were still bold.

Once you get to know your toddler, you'll begin to get an idea of his temperament and the things that he likes and doesn't like. Although you shouldn't pigeonhole your child, it is helpful and sensitive to understand and make allowances for your toddler's temperament. This is true if he is shy and timid and is also true if he is bold or clumsy. All toddlers will experience anxiety and fear but if you learn what situations or stimuli (e.g. loud dogs) make your toddler fearful you can begin to help him to overcome fears and build his confidence in you and in himself. Older siblings can also (with some supervision) be great role models who can gently challenge your toddler to face a fear.

real parent story

Polly (Ava, 2 years)

'I notice balloons at 50 paces because of Ava's balloon phobia. I think one must have popped when she was about one as ever

since she gets clingy and cries. At first I'd just get rid of the balloon or take her away, but with parties and what have you it was hard to avoid them. So my Mum has started showing her empty balloons and blowing them up a tiny bit and letting them slowly go down. She's much better now but she's still a bit wary of them which is a shame as balloons are great ... until they pop!'

Quiz: Is my toddler bold or cautious?

1. You show your toddler a loud flashing toy. Does he:
   a) Run towards it and pick it up.
   b) Look to you for reassurance and then approach the toy cautiously.
   c) Show fear of the toy and stay with you.

2. At a toddler music group, does your toddler:
   a) Choose the loudest instrument and jump around happily in the middle of the group.
   b) Prefer to sit on your knee for the class, holding his chosen instrument.
   c) Get upset with the noise and may even cry and want to leave the class.

3. When a stranger talks to your toddler does he:
   a) Respond and keep talking to the stranger, perhaps showing off and being loud and excited.
   b) Look to reassurance before answering the stranger's questions with short answers.
   c) Avoid the stranger's gaze and come back to you for reassurance.

4. You ask your toddler to reach into a box with a hole. Does he:
   a) Reach straight in unfazed and enjoy pulling out the contents of the box.

    b) Need some reassurance and will put his hands in the box
       with you.

    c) Be very anxious and refuse to put his hands in or near the
       box.

5. You offer your toddler a new fruit to taste. Does he:
    a) Take a bite straight away.
    b) Need some reassurance and may take a small bite.
    c) Refuse to try the fruit

6. How does your toddler cope with strong smells, e.g. bleach?
   (sign of a sensitive amygdala)
    a) He doesn't seem to notice.
    b) He may show a disgust face.
    c) He wrinkles up his nose and may even gag.

7. You take your toddler to a firework display. Does he:
    a) Grin from ear to ear and seem entranced with the loud
       noises and bright lights.
    b) Want to stay close to you and prefer the quieter fireworks.
       He may not want to watch a very long display.
    c) Show real fear and cry and cling to you until he's taken
       away from the display.

Mostly As: Your toddler displays lots of bold behaviour in a variety of situations and with different stimuli. He is not behaviourally inhibited.

Mostly Bs: Your toddler is neither very bold nor very timid. He social references you and uses you as a secure base to give him confidence with new experiences.

Mostly Cs: Your toddler displays anxiety around a variety of novel situations and stimuli. He is somewhat behaviourally inhibited and his amygdala is probably sensitive to loud noises, strong smells and 'scary' situations.

TOP TIP

If your toddler refuses to attempt a physical feat such as climb a new climbing frame, you need to respect that. Do not force him or bribe him. Instead, adapt the feat next time so it is less scary, such as just climbing the ladder and then back down again. Once he has mastered that, you can try to increase the challenge a little more each time.

mine! sharing and taking turns

'You are forgiven for your happiness and your successes only if you generously consent to share them.'

Albert Camus

Psychologists use a phrase, 'theory of mind', to describe the ability of human beings to put themselves in the shoes of another person. Not only does this allow us to empathise and care for people, but it also allows us to read people and social situations.

This 'mind-reading' ability does not tend to develop until three to five years of age; your toddler's under-developed brain literally makes her single-minded, more egocentric and, for want of a better word, selfish.

FALSE-BELIEF TASKS

Psychologists have used so-called 'false-belief tasks' to help observe when children develop the ability to understand what knowledge another person has. Gaining the ability to understand false beliefs is a huge milestone in a child's mind development.

The most well used false-belief task in psychology is the 'Sally-Anne' test. Children are told a story (often with puppets and props) about Sally and Anne. Sally has a basket that she puts her marble in and Anne has a box.

When Sally leaves the room, Anne removes the marble from Sally's basket and puts it in her box. Sally returns. The child is then asked where Sally will look for her marble. A child 'passes' the test if she realises that Sally will look in her basket (even though she has a false belief that it is still there and doesn't realise that it has been moved to the box).

A child 'fails' the task if she states that Sally will look in the box (where the child knows the marble is now). This means to pass the Sally-Anne test a child must be able to understand that another person's mental representation of the situation is different from their own (even though it's wrong); from this understanding she must be able to predict how a person with a false belief will therefore behave.

TEST – FALSE–BELIEF TASK

Take a bar of chocolate and put it on a shelf. Let your toddler's teddy bear see the chocolate and then take the teddy out of the room. Once the teddy is out of the room take the chocolate bar to the fridge with your toddler and put it into the fridge. Then bring teddy back into the room and ask your toddler where teddy will look for the chocolate bar. To pass the task, your toddler would need to understand that the teddy bear holds 'false belief' that the chocolate bar is still on the shelf.

I would expect that your toddler will not pass this test because she is too young and this is entirely normal. I hope that by carrying out this false-belief test on your toddler it will allow you to empathise and realise the thinking power that she is currently equipped with. Much of her apparent 'selfishness' comes out of this inability to put herself in another's shoes.

Although the ability to fully 'pass' a false-belief task doesn't occur before the age of three or so fantastic research by Professor Alison Gopnik at Berkley University in California has shown that development of theory of mind is not like a light switching on. A toddler will begin to appreciate other people's preferences from around 18 months.

Gopnik set up an experiment where toddlers were asked for food. The toddlers watched while the experimenter expressed disgust when she ate one food and said 'yum yum' and smiled with another food. The experimenter then asked the toddler for something to eat from the food offered. The experiment was designed to see if toddlers could predict which food the experimenter would prefer and give it to them.

The 14-month-old toddlers were egocentric and simply gave the experimenter the food that they preferred themselves. However, by 18 months, the toddlers correctly gave the experimenter the food that they had previously said 'yum yum' to, even if it wasn't the toddler's preference.

Gopnik termed this first ability to understand another person might have a different preference as 'desire reasoning'. The 18-month-old toddlers could hold in their heads that another person had a different desire to them and that it was communicated by facial expressions and sounds.

Your toddler's largely egocentric brain is completely central to understanding your toddler's limited view of the world and the people in it. Your toddler does not have the brain development to fully put themselves inside someone else's mind (though they have an understanding that facial expressions give information about that person's feelings). Once you acknowledge this truth about your toddler you will feel more forgiving of your toddler's selfishness. This helps us to understand why toddlers have such problems sharing – they just don't realise that everyone else shares their strong preference to have things their own way.

However, Gopnik's research shows that your toddler is already empathic at only 18 months of age and is using facial expressions and verbal communication (or delight or disgust) to understand another person's preferences. You can help to develop and promote your toddler's empathy to help lead their cognitive development of theory of mind.

How to encourage sharing and turn-taking

Taking turns and sharing is not something that comes naturally to toddlers. As your toddler develops a stronger sense of will, she will be outraged if a toy is taken away from her and, from around 18 months, will immediately want it back. If the toy is taken by another toddler things can quickly escalate.

Make sure there are plenty of toys to share and in a gentle way you may need to police the sharing of toys and fair turn-taking. If you consistently explain that 'everyone wants a go of the toy so we need to take turns' they will begin to see that the system does work in their favour too. They don't always lose something, just as often they will get a turn.

real parent story

George (Marley, 4 years and Noah, 30 months)

'My two were totally different. Marley's favourite word was 'mine' and going to the park was a bit stressy as he wanted to hog the swing or the mini roundabout. I would let him have a go and then count him down from 10 to 1 then say 'Blast off! Now it's the little girl's turn.' He had lots of meltdowns but I persevered. Noah has the other problem in that if a child comes towards him he gives them the toy straight away, not sure if it's because he has a big brother who doesn't share well. I try and do the same thing, say it's his turn to play with it and then count down and say now you can see if the girl wants a go. Talk about chalk and cheese.'

OLIVE AND CRACKER TEST

This is a fun test to try with your toddler and an adult to observe your child's ability to understand another person's preference.

Ask the adult to taste from a bowl of food your toddler doesn't like (e.g. olives) and from a bowl of something you know your toddler loves (e.g. crackers). When the adult eats the olives she needs to do a big 'yum yum' and smile. When the adult eats the crackers she needs to do a big 'yuk' and pull a face of utter disgust.

Then place the bowls in front of your toddler. Your friend needs to hold out her hand and ask for some food.

Under 18 months old your toddler will probably offer her the crackers (or her favourite food) but at 18 months your toddler will understand that your friend has a different prefer-ence to her and will accordingly offer your friend the olives. If you are concerned about putting her off olives you can make sure that you and other people around her happily eat the olives or use a non-food example, e.g. a favoured toy and an unfavoured toy.

TOP TIP

At the park it can help to instil a rule that each toddler gets so many goes. I would always explain to one of my toddlers that he or she would get 30 swings on the swing and then swap. My toddlers and their friends were much more accepting of turn-taking if the turns were quick and being monitored in a way they could begin to understand.

chapter twelve

now! instant gratification

'Instant gratification takes too long.'

Mae West

Toddlers certainly can't be accused of dithering over decisions. One of the first powerful statements (after 'no!') you
will hear your toddler say is, 'now!'

In order to plan and think about the future you need a fully
developed neo cortex, or frontal lobe. This brain structure isn't
fully developed in toddlers and so they find it impossible to
delay gratification – they simply don't have the hardware. It isn't
until the age of three that the first inklings of this ability begin
to surface.

This was first reported in the now-famous 1960s marshmallow test by Walter Mischel. He asked four-year-old children if
they'd like one marshmallow then added, 'If you don't eat it
until I get back you can have two.' There was a big range in
behaviour, with some children immediately gobbling up the
sweet, whilst others employed tactics to help them wait. The
interesting tactic used by the children who could wait, was that
they side-tracked themselves to take their focus away from the
delicious marshmallow. They walked and danced around the
marshmallow until the psychologists came back.

Unlike many four-year-olds toddlers have very limited ability to
delay gratification and it can really help to instead side-track them
from whatever is overwhelmingly desirable now. For example,
try 'Let's see if we can find your teddy bear so he can have some
ice cream too.' Side-tracking is a powerful trick in your arsenal
of helping to manage your toddler's tantrums, impulses and

emotions. This is because your toddler's emotions and thoughts can be very ephemeral and fast-running. You can help to move your toddler's focus and emotion on by drawing his attention to something exciting or positive; this can literally be about anything; a cat walking along a fence, the moon in the sky during the day or even a well-timed question that helps your toddler to move his attention away from the source of frustration.

The marshmallow researcher went on to find that those children in his study who were able to delay gratification were more likely to develop resilience and tenacity in later life. Although we can't expect toddlers to be very good at delaying gratification, we can always help them to have little practices to train the muscle. This can be as simple as getting him in the habit of eating cake after his main meal (which is better for dental health) or feed the dog before they go to the park. This helps your toddler to see time in bite-sized pieces and have a greater sense of what's happening now and then what will happen next.

However, my main take home point is that, as parents, we should have compassion when faced with a toddler's inability to delay gratification. Whilst we might pride ourselves as grown-ups on holding off eating a treat until after dinner, we adults can be very gluttonous when it comes to things like box sets of top drama series. We put our toddlers to sleep and then gorge on perhaps three or four episodes in one go. Try and remember this when you get frustrated with your toddler's ejaculations of 'now!' and 'more!'

How brain development affects toddler behaviour

Unlike toddlers, adults have a fully functioning frontal cortex which allows us to plan and make decisions, as well as having memories that reinforce our understanding that delaying something can actually benefit us. Toddlers are only just beginning to lay down memories of when delaying gratification paid off. They are at the beginning of a long journey that we all face to learn to control our impulses. As parents we can help them by modelling good impulse control ourselves, e.g. not mainlining through an entire packet of biscuits in one go.

As you would expect from the name, the frontal lobe of the brain sits behind the forehead. The frontal lobe (or frontal cortex) processes all our conscious thoughts and voluntary behaviour, so the frontal lobe is actively 'in control' when we are talking, painting and solving a problem like a jigsaw. Your toddler's frontal lobe began to develop between six and 12 months, and drives his communication and physical development.

The frontal lobe doesn't fully mature until 30 years of age, and slightly regresses in the teenage years, which may explain why some teenagers seem to behave a little like toddlers with increased impulsivity, lack of planning and risky behaviour.

---

real parent story

Helen (Lewis, 6 years)

'I remember Lewis being so desperate to have a Happy Meal toy when he was about three, and I was explaining that we had to get the shopping first and then we'd drive there on the way home. In an attempt to win his case for a Happy Meal toy now he got flustered and frustrated and said, 'because ... because ... because ... McDonalds!'

DELAY OF GRATIFICATION –
THE MARSHMALLOW TEST

The point of this test is to illustrate how limited your toddler's ability to delay gratification is, so you can understand how he manages gratification and waiting. You can do this famous test with any treat you like, such as chocolate buttons or strawberries.

Put the treat on a plate on a low table and explain to your toddler that he can eat the treat if he wants but if he waits until you come back he can have two treats. Leave the room, but try and observe if possible, to supervise and see his coping strategy. Return in two to five minutes (though Mischel waited up to 20 minutes).

Does your child choose to eat the immediate treat or wait so he can have two? If he waited tell him he did really well waiting for you and give him the extra treat. If he didn't wait, explain that next time, if he can wait, he will get double the treats. Most children, up to the age of four years, will eat the single treat.

TOP TIP

Toddlers don't have a good handle on the concept of time, so, instead of saying he can paint in ten minutes, put it into a context he will understand. For example, 'We can get the paints out after we have fed the cat and I've washed the dishes.'

chapter thirteen

didn't! fibbing, lying and hiding

'Children and fools tell the truth.'

English Proverb

Let's be honest, the vast majority of adults lie on a daily or weekly basis. These may be white lies, a slight massaging of the truth, or lies that get us out of 'trouble' or to get an outcome we want. Lying is not something adults are proud of or something we want to have to contend with in our children, which is why we get very judgemental and upset when our children lie.

However, lying is a universal stage in your child's development and it is actually a sign that your toddler is developing cognitively. This means that a child that lies understands that the recipient of the lie has less knowledge of the facts than she does. This is a huge step and something that separates us from most animals.

Your toddler will probably begin to tell her first fibs soon after her second birthday. With her limited vocabulary, theory of mind (see page 151) and mental concepts, the first lies are usually simple denials. So when asked outright if she has done something 'wrong' she will begin to say 'no' as they understand that certain behaviours are frowned upon and associated with parental disapproval. However, the subterfuge is very limited – as soon as you ask follow-up questions she will be unable to maintain her story.

In a straw poll of my friends, nearly all of their toddlers had at one time covered themselves in Sudocrem nappy cream and then (whilst basted in the stuff), solemnly announced it wasn't them!

By the time your toddler is three her social and emotional development has led to an increase in noticing 'polite' behaviour and an increased, though limited, empathy with others. She might be able to tell a white lie, especially if she is coached to, for example, 'If Aunty Sally comes here please say you like her new hair colour as she's a bit upset about it.' Your toddler will be the weak link in the chain but she may also be able to briefly withhold exciting surprise information, e.g. that her Mother's Day card is hidden in her bedroom, until the morning ... but it will be tough.

Your toddler's fibbing 'skills' will increase as her cognitive development increases, her social and emotional development increases, and her language acquisition develops.

Lying and theory of mind

Lying relies on a human ability called 'theory of mind' (see page 151). Having theory of mind means that a person is able to put themselves in the mind and perspective of another person. It's very easy to see that your toddler struggles with this concept when she plays hide and seek. There are whole Tumblr accounts devoted to hilarious hide-and-seek toddler 'fails':

- toddlers lying face down on the ground in the middle of a room
- toddlers standing behind the curtains with their legs sticking out at the bottom
- toddlers putting their head behind a small cushion.

All of these toddlers think that because *they* can't see the seeker, *they* can't be seen. They have no concept or ability to imagine what the seeker can see. It is only that we find this mental gymnastics so effortless that we find toddler hide-and-seek so funny and ridiculous!

Theory of mind starts to develop at around three and a half years, generally earlier in girls than boys and never in many children with severe autism. From this age children begin to realise that other people have their own knowledge about the world, although they develop an understanding that other people have different preferences to them from as early as 18 months.

Having 'theory of mind' is effortless for us but it's an incredibly sophisticated mental ability as you need to be able to 'get inside' another person's head and see their point of view... and then exploit it to your own benefit. It is only when this conceptual ability matures that Machiavellian manipulation can occur. As children become more able to think about what other people think and feel, they learn when it's appropriate to lie and how to lie convincingly, but it's a slow process.

Although lying is a sign of huge leaps in your child's cognitive and emotional development we all generally want to encourage our children to be truthful and honest.

If you are fair but firm and always praise your toddler for telling the truth she will reward you with more honesty. She will more easily internalise your rules and boundaries as they are fair, and come from a warm and loving parent.

You can encourage a culture of honesty in your home by having a warm and sensitive attitude. Draconian punishments, such as the naughty step and smacking for accidents like spilling drinks and hurting siblings arguably lead to strategies of denial and secrecy.

There is scientific evidence that punishing lying doesn't work. One study carried out by Cindy Arruda, Sarah Yachison and Victoria Talwar at McGill University in Canada perfectly illustrated the responses of children to punishment for lying and appeals for truthfulness. They developed a 'temptation resistance test' whereby a noisy toy was placed behind the child subject. They then said that the child was not allowed to peek. With the huge temptation, around four-fifths of the children peeked.

The interesting results came with the children when they were asked if they had peeked or not. If asked point blank, 67.5 per cent of children who peeked lied, and said they didn't peek. Interestingly, if the children were threatened with sanction if they did peek, this increased the chances of lying. With or without the threat of punishment they found that without an appeal to tell the truth, more than 80 per cent of the children lied.

Another group had appeals for honesty; one group was told by the researcher: 'I will feel happy if you tell the truth,' and the other honesty group was told: 'Telling the truth is the right thing to do.'

Half of the children that were told that telling the truth would make the researcher happy chose to then tell the truth regardless of whether they thought they would be punished or not. Saying that telling the truth was the moral thing to do reduced lying to 40 per cent in the group that didn't expect punishment (it remained twice as high in the group that did expect punishment). Professor Talwar summarised the findings:

> What seems to increase honesty is giving children explicit messages about the value of honesty. If we wish to teach children to act in prosocial ways, we need to teach children about those behaviours and why they are important. We need to teach children about the value of being honest. When a child does something wrong a natural reaction is to punish their transgression. However, if they tell the truth about it, we can give them some recognition for it. 'I'm not happy you broke my vase – and you can help me clean it up/fix it/use your pocket money to replace it – but I'm glad you told me the truth.' If we recognise honesty that is a powerful way to encourage and teach children that honesty is valued.

real parent story

Debbie (Ben, 4 years)

'Ben is such a fibber and it does worry me a bit as he seems to do it to gain approval, so if someone is talking about Superman, Ben will say he's seen Superman, or whatever, to kind of show-off. I think it's slightly my fault as I didn't want to criticise him when he was telling a tall tale so would be like 'Wow, really!' I've now started to try and say that he doesn't need to exaggerate and that people won't believe him if he tells fibs but I find it tricky as I don't want to dampen his imagination completely.'

TEST – HIDE-AND-SEEK

This is a simple test – play hide-and-seek with your toddler, both with her hiding and letting her hide something small from you. You may find that she is able to hide a small thing from you more easily than hiding herself. Over time you will see your child will get better at hide-and-seek as they begin to be able to put themselves in the mind of the 'seeker'.

TOP TIP

Research has shown that the best way to encourage honesty is by reassuring your child that she won't be in trouble if she tells the truth and also that it would make you happy. If you want to encourage honesty you need to explain to your toddler that you understand that accidents happen, or that everyone gets angry sometimes, and then in that moment of shared experience ask her to tell you what happened.

chapter fourteen

ouch! risk-taking

'The human heart was not designed to beat outside the human body and yet, each child represented just that – a parent's heart bared, beating forever outside its chest.'

Debra Ginsberg, *Raising Blaze*

Your toddler's antics will sometimes leave you with your heart in your mouth. Toddlers aren't very good or experienced at assessing risk or anticipating danger. This means they need lots of supervision and you need to make sure that your home is toddler-proof and that the environments your toddler plays in are safe from dangers.

However, toddlers should not be wrapped in cotton wool, and, where possible, they should have the freedom to balance, climb, paddle, get messy and safely interact with animals. This is how they will learn to assess and take appropriate risks in life.

When your toddler is playing or exploring, try not to blurt out, 'Be careful, be careful', as this is just an anxiety-inducing alert without offering specific guidance. Instead, explain, 'This hill is slippery so let's take our time.'

In one study, anxious mums (as assessed by questionnaires of general anxiety about life) were reported to say 'be careful', and generally highlight risks significantly more frequently than non-anxious mums. Their children went on to become more anxious. Whilst we cannot conclude this is a direct cause-and-effect relationship, it can really help to think about the language we use about risk and danger around our children.

Quiz: Are you an anxious parent?

Even the most laid back adult often experiences the first jolt of real anxiety when they become a parent. Loving a precious and seemingly vulnerable child makes all parents a 'hostage to fortune'. However, some parents become so extremely anxious about their toddler that they can smother them. Try the following quiz to see if you may be an anxious parent and see the top tips to help you regulate and reign in your anxiety and need to control things.

1. Your child says that his head hurts. Do you:
   a) Tell him to stop moaning, there's nothing wrong.
   b) Keep an eye on him and see if he mentions having a sore head again.
   c) Worry that your child has a life-threatening condition and get onto Google.

2. You have taken your child to a paint-a-pot gallery. Do you:
   a) Let him choose what he wants to paint, leave him to it and grab a coffee.
   b) Show him a couple of simple pots to paint and help him get together all the paints he needs and sit and talk with him as he daubs away.
   c) Choose the pot you like best and help him paint so it will look nice.

3. Your baby has discovered the stairs. Do you:
   a) Let him experiment and climb up and down. If he takes a tumble he'll learn more quickly.
   b) Let him have supervised time climbing up the stairs with you behind but have stair gates closed otherwise.
   c) Tell him 'no!' or 'dangerous!' and keep him away from the stairs.

4. Your toddler hits another toddler at a party in front of all the other parents. Do you:
   a) Pretend not to notice. Toddlers are always rough and they need to be left to sort things out between them.

b) Go to the hurt toddler and say: 'Oh, are you okay?' and then calmly talk to your toddler explaining that we don't hit other people as it hurts.

c) Loudly tell your toddler hitting is not acceptable and if he doesn't say sorry you will leave the party ... and stick to your guns.

5. When you think about your baby's future do you:
a) I don't think about the future – I live in the moment and try to enjoy now.

b) Feel part-excited about what he will be like and what he will do with his life, but also worry about his future.

c) Constantly think of all the dangers and uncertainties he will face and worry that you cannot protect him.

Mostly As: You are so relaxed you are horizontal. However, your toddler might feel more secure with more guidance, more limits and fewer preventable accidents.

Mostly Bs: You worry like every parent but you try not to sweat the small stuff. You make sure your child is safe from unnecessary harm and feels guided by your loving support.

Mostly Cs: You spend a lot of time worrying about everything. Try to enjoy your time with your toddler. This is good for you both. Try to see his life as an exciting journey with more ups than downs.

Dealing with your own anxiety

Anxiety is a natural part of being a parent. When you drive home from the hospital with your 'little bundle' you suddenly realise that you are completely responsible for this little person. It's no wonder that countless parents have crept up to their sleeping child to double-check he is breathing, or spent the entire visit to the park telling their boisterous toddler to, 'be careful!'

But where do the natural feelings of concern spill into something that is stressful for the parent and suffocating for the child? Anxiety tends to run in families; this is, in part, due to a genetic inheritance of anxious tendencies, but children also 'learn' to be anxious from being around an anxious parent and become anxious because of the way their parent makes them feel.

I completed a PhD to assess the impact of the parenting style of anxious mums (in comparison to mums who were rated and self-rated as low-anxiety). In my research I gave mums lots of tasks and drawing games to play with their children in a laboratory setting. In every task the anxious mums were very different from the non-anxious mums. Whereas the more relaxed mums were warm and praising, the mums with high anxiety levels were critical and controlling and the task was no fun for anyone. See also page 145 on the 'scary things' project.

Similarly in a potentially 'stressful' task I brought a big black box into the room with a hole in the top and asked the mums to encourage their children to lift out the 'scary things' from the bottom of the box.

Most of the children didn't want to put their hand in the box regardless of what kind of mum they had! However, the non-anxious mums were not scared of the box themselves and didn't make their child put their hand into the box. Instead they were a model of calm and said things like, 'I know, you hold my hand while I put my other hand in the box!' They put their child first, made it fun and didn't force their child to pull things out of the box.

The anxious mums were very different. They were scared of putting their own hand in the box ... whilst at the same time insisting that their child lift out the rubber creepy crawlies!

In general, psychologists have found that anxious mums are more likely to be critical of their children, worry what people think, and display more fear and anxiety in common situations.

All these behaviours are more likely to instil fear and low confidence in their own children. This goes some way to explain why anxiety runs in families, though anxious tendencies are inherited too. If you feel that anxiety is taking over your life you should speak to your GP and you can visit www.mind.org to find out more about anxiety and how to help yourself.

How to boost your child's confidence

As well as trying to reduce how you communicate your own anxieties to your child, there are other ways to reduce anxiety and boost self-confidence in your child. These are my 'five Ps'.

Play

Children learn through play. Let your toddler have a go at something first himself, and try not to micro-manage what he tries to do. Toddlers live in the moment and love to try new things.

Praise

Everyone responds well to praise. Praise your child when he tries things, and especially praise persistence and hard work. Don't just praise the end result as children do not care about the end result so much, e.g., 'you are putting lots of red paint on the picture, it's very bright and pretty' rather than 'Oh have you made a flower, it looks great.'

Pretend

If you want to avoid passing on some of your own phobias or worries try to be brave for your child. Children look to their parents to guide how they should feel or behave in certain situations and will model their parents' behaviour. Even if you are not keen on snakes or spiders, try to be as calm and reassuring as you can for your child so that he doesn't learn to respond with fear and anxiety too.

Personality

All children are different, some fearless and some cautious (see page 124). All parents will get to know their own child and be able to gauge their comfort zone around certain things. Try to be reassuring and encouraging but avoid forcing your toddler to do things that he finds very frightening. Forcing them could result in him becoming more withdrawn and feeling less in control. So respect their personality and take things gently.

Performance

Try not to worry about your 'performance' as a parent. Most parents feel under pressure to be seen to parent in a certain way in public. Try to focus on the real relationship with your child and deal with situations in the way you know works with you and your child.

Social referencing and risk

Your toddler is very bad at assessing risk in the home and when out and about. Luckily toddlers have evolved 'social referencing' behaviour to help decide whether something is dangerous based on their care-givers facial expression. This means that your facial expressions, gestures and words are important in helping your toddler to develop risk assessment skills.

This might mean encouraging your toddler with a big smile and a 'thumbs-up' when he approaches something new, and contrast with 'danger' signals when he is doing something dangerous.

Make sure that you don't 'cry wolf' and endlessly communicate fear about the littlest thing. Get used to getting your toddler's attention when he is playing at a distance from you, and communicate the risk level to him with your words, gestures and facial expressions.

Famous experiments pioneered by Joseph Campos at Berkeley University of California revealed the role of social referencing in infant development. Campos created a 'visual cliff', which was a laboratory environment of a safe plane of glass placed over a chequered floor to create the illusion that there was a big drop in the middle of the room.

The experiment demonstrated that older toddlers were afraid of the drop, though they could sometimes cross the drop if their mothers smiled and encouraged them to cross towards them. If a mother showed a fearful face their toddler was significantly less likely to cross the drop. In short, they were swayed by the emotional communication and facial expressions of someone they trusted implicitly – their mum. This phenomenon was called 'social referencing'.

Impulsive behaviour

Complete silence, calm and quiet is frequently associated with your toddler utterly engrossed in an impulsive behaviour that often means mess and sometimes means danger. So, as you inwardly cheer that your toddler is very quiet – check him out immediately. Hopefully it will just be a silly or messy game but sometimes their impulsivity and lack of judgement can lead to dangerous behaviours. A friend of mine checked on her quiet toddler to discover she had pulled a chair to an open window and was standing on the windowsill looking out. Thankfully she was calmly able to lift down her toddler, and the next day install window locks throughout the home. These near-misses haunt many parents.

Many toddlers go through a quite frightening stage of bolting. This is usually when he is first learning to run and he is like a 'wind-up' toy when you put him down. Toddlers in our family have run into ponds, into the road, and into crowds in shopping centres. Supervision during the toddler years has to be very high. Sadly, you have to accept that you can't drop your guard when your toddler is going through a running and bolting phase.

Your toddler is too young to be sensible, so one good way to prevent bolting leading to a bad accident is to take your toddler to really big open spaces, such as a fenced play area, beach or common. Another great boon for parents today are the well-designed soft play centres that allow intrepid toddlers to run off energy and to explore, climb, and bolt to their hearts' content.

Holding hands and reins

Toddlers love to be independent and might prefer not to hold hands, which can be potentially fatal on busy roads. In this case you have to be firm and say that he either holds your hand or he has to sit in the pram or be carried until you are away from the busy road. However, I hate to see toddlers cooped up in a buggy for an entire shopping trip, and it is usually possible to give them the opportunity to run off some steam, which I think is only fair.

I have had some success with backpacks that have a little lead on them, which lets you walk with your toddler without constant hand-holding. Reins such as this can also prevent some bad falls, but in general I only used them near busy roads.

---

real parent story

Mark (Rebecca and Jessica, both 28 months)

'I was always a pretty relaxed dad until I had the twins and my nerves just couldn't take them both bolting in opposite direc-tions. At the park I'd push Rebecca in the swing and let Jessica

toddle around and then swap them over, that way I could dash after one of them and the other one couldn't bolt too. We got them those backpacks with little leads but it was a bit of a battle but I was really firm when we were near roads – either sit in the pram or have your backpack on.'

TOP TIP

If you struggle with letting your toddler take acceptable risks, you could try going with a 'braver' or more relaxed partner or friend. Let them take control of the playing so you get to see your toddler supported but trying some new things that are riskier than you normally allow. I learned this inadvertently with my youngest daughter. Her best friend's mum whizzed them around on a piece of equipment that required them to hang on tight. She would spin it as high as possible. My heart was in my mouth, but my daughter loved it and I learned to increase the risks that my 'baby' could take.

part three

common hurdles

In this third part of the book you will learn how to manage and parent your toddler through the most common hurdles that all toddlers need help with, including potty learning, sleep and tantrums.

toddler 'manners'

'Correcting bad habits cannot be done by forbidding or punishment.'

Robert Baden-Powell

I always think it must have been very difficult having a toddler in the Victorian era as certain classes were so repressed and so much behaviour was frowned on. Probably one of the reasons for the separate nursery with a nanny in the upper classes was that toddlers were only brought into public, or indeed in the presence of their parents, for short, controlled periods of time where they were clean, not eating and were fully dressed to minimise any unpleasant public behaviour.

Thankfully we now live in a more accepting and realistic society that makes allowances for the fact that toddlers are not miniature adults and experts in etiquette. However, good manners are an important part of development and slowly, gently and firmly you will need to explain the boundaries of acceptable and unacceptable behaviour.

Nose-picking

Toddlers are naturally curious and will explore their nostrils in the same way they might explore a burrow in the ground. Toddlers are also uninhibited, because they are essentially egocentric and are not aware that they are observed by other people. They also are not yet steeped in the cultural expectations about their bodies. Nose-picking is considered unpleasant across most cultures as disgust at contagious bodily fluids like snot, vomit and poo has an instinctive basis.

However, if anyone has something stuck up their nose it's very tempting to try and remove it. Adults learn to control it (in public at least, unless they are in a traffic jam!) but toddlers will be very interested in their nostrils. You may also find that your toddler goes through a phase of putting things inside orifices such as her nose, ears and in some cases their anus and/ or vagina.

I had to take my son to the accident and emergency room once when he pushed a green pompom up his nose. I was reassured as an embarrassed parent to hear that this was a daily job of the casualty staff, as a nurse expertly removed the green pompom with a pair of tweezers.

Lots of nose-picking can lead to bleeding and scabs so if your toddler is a dedicated nose-picker you will need to try to teach her to blow her nose instead. However, even school children find this really hard to do, so you will need to help her close a nostril and blow into a tissue until she can control the out breath through her nose herself.

Masturbation

Toddlers enjoy lots of sensations, whether it be playing in sand, water or running on grass. Most psychologists today would agree that when toddlers play with their genitals it is simply because it feels pleasant and they are positively rewarded physiologically.

The main problem for parents is that it is embarrassing if their toddler plays with herself in public. It often becomes more of a public problem when your toddler graduates from nappies to underpants and has easy access to her nether regions. Some parents also worry that it is some kind of sexual deviance, but it is pretty much universal toddler behaviour across cultures and genders because toddlers are not yet inhibited by social mores.

Try not to get upset about your toddler's explorations of her own body and gently let her know that 'we keep our hands out of our trousers when we are at the shops'. If anyone has been to a nativity play at a nursery there is generally at least one shepherd with his hands inside his smock, such is the prevalence of this behaviour.

If you have family members who are particularly embarrassed when your toddler explores her body in this way, you can always choose clothes for that day that make getting her hands into her underpants more difficult, such as dungarees or tights and a pinafore dress.

Don't be ashamed of your toddler and don't make her feel ashamed or disgusted by her behaviour as this will confuse and upset her. With gentle distractions and reminders about public fiddling, this behaviour will soon become a past phase.

Swearing

Toddlers are language machines and any swearing they do is swearing they've heard. It can therefore be mortifying if your toddler swears in public or in front of relatives. However, remember she is not being naughty; she is being a parrot.

One story that always makes me laugh was my niece. My dad was retired and looked after my niece during the day when she was a toddler. Her baby brother's car seat was on the floor in the sitting room and she was kneeling down in front of the seat putting in her teddy bear and putting the straps over its shoulders. As she came to doing up the three-way buckle at the front she started banging them together loudly repeating, 'bubby ell, bubby ell!' My mum watched with incomprehension until the penny dropped. My dad always struggled with the three-way buckle and as he tried to fix it he would curse 'bloody hell' throughout.

What I find particularly funny and touching is that my niece, like all toddlers, was so observant and such a good copier that she obviously believed that an important part of shutting the harness was the mantra 'bubby ell, bubby ell.'

Not all swearing is charming however. I also remember my angelic eldest daughter innocently asking my mum to push her higher on the swing adding 'you f*cker'. I don't know where it came from (though must admit that that word does drop from my lips on occasion). My mum laughed out of shock and genuine amusement at the juxtaposition of the innocent bonny toddler uttering such a rude word. Of course, when she laughed my socially intelligent toddler loved the positive response and that phrase was flavour of the day. With a concerted effort at us not reacting she moved onto something else quite quickly.

Toddlers will copy sounds and words as part of learning language. If your toddler hears swearing she will swear, so remember that when you get cut up at a junction whilst driving and try to remain calm. I know that my middle child hated to hear me being angry in the car; he had no clue what it was about and just felt my negative tone and anger. He didn't have the theory of mind (see page 151) to realise that I was looking out of my windscreen and shouting at people he couldn't see and didn't know existed. To him I was shouting 'at' him, and once I realised this I made an effort to chill out in the car and avoid the swearing, anger and any aggressive driving attitudes. Of course the positive feedback to me was lovely and car rides became much better for everyone involved; other road users, me and my anxious toddler!

Refusing to kiss older relatives

Although it is embarrassing when your toddler is unsociable or non-complying with requests for kisses and cuddles for extended family members, it is not fair to force them. Even at this early stage in life consent to kissing and cuddling is important and should be respected.

Your toddler may be going through a period of separation anxiety or increased fear of strangers. Forcing a fearful child to kiss a stranger on the lips or sit on their knee or play with them isn't a fair request really. Sometimes they will be happy to kiss or cuddle a relative but don't turn it into a battle of wills as it will be more embarrassing and upsetting than simply telling your great-aunt that your toddler is a bit shy of new people at the minute.

Pointing at people who are different

Being out and about with a toddler in public can be a little stressful when your toddler notices someone who looks different from other people. In the fairy tale of *The Emperor's New Clothes*, it is no accident that the person who announced that the emperor was naked was a small child!

Toddlers have no idea about other people's feelings so if your toddler announces loudly: 'Why has that person got pink hair?' she has no idea that a person might find it embarrassing to be singled out in public. In the same way, toddlers do not feel disgusted or angry with 'different' people, they just notice them.

I remember that I had been asked by my friend to look after her toddler in a shop while she ran upstairs to check out the baby clothes. A very small woman came into the shop, and my friend's daughter noticed her, pointed at her and said repeatedly: 'Tiny lady! Tiny lady! Tiny lady!' I was mortified and the woman was embarrassed (more by my obvious embarrassment I expect) and in true English-style we didn't know quite what to do.

People who do stand out, whether it is because they have a facial disfigurement, or are an unusual size or shape, usually report that they have no problem with the brutal honesty of toddlers. Rather, it's the behaviour of adults and older children that they feel is cruel – people who should and do know better. How can a toddler be cruel when they are not motivated by malice at all?

The wonderful thing about children is actually their lack of judgement of different people. They may perceive a difference but they quickly accept it, whether it is a child at their playgroup with a physical or mental disability, that child will just be Jack who has a wheelchair.

In your day-to-day chats with your toddler you can explain that some people look different and that it is important to be kind and explain not to say things like a person looks 'funny' as it will hurt their feelings. Over time, children who are taught to think about other people's feelings in general will more quickly behave with kindness and understanding.

real parent story

Eleanor (Damian, 9 years, Kieran, 6 years and Eira, 4 years)

'All my children have gone through a phase of fiddling with themselves when they were toddlers and pre-schoolers. I didn't want to be uptight about it as it seems a natural extension of learning about their own bodies. I generally ignored it at home and sometimes would say 'stop fiddling with yourself, no one wants to see that'. The phase seems to have passed but I expect it will return in the teenage years!'

TOP TIP

Accept that you will have to take the rough with the smooth as the parent of a toddler, and that one day your toddler will utterly embarrass and mortify you. But it's more about adults not toddlers; they are not mean-spirited, just developing.

chapter sixteen

dummies, thumb-sucking and other props

'In the absence of any other proof, the thumb alone would convince me of God's existence.'

Isaac Newton

Sucking seems to be an extremely prevalent self-soothing behaviour with babies in the womb often seen to be sucking their thumb during scans. It is no surprise to see that thumb sucking and dummy-sucking are such beloved and deep-rooted habits.

As a toddler I sucked my thumb and cuddled and sniffed my revolting piece of brushed cotton called my 'gummy'. Oh how I loved my gummy and my thumb-sucking was so relentless that I even developed an infected thumb once.

Dummies

Dummies are not universal props but they are used a lot in the West to soothe babies. My babies were all premature and although they were able to breastfeed and had a good sucking response they tended to spit out any dummy that was offered to them, but I know that some babies are very sucky and love their dummy.

Pros and cons of dummy use

Two meta-studies (studies comparing lots of studies) by the Cochrane Collaboration concluded that dummies do not interfere with breastfeeding with mums who are determined to breastfeed and in fact may protect babies from SIDS (Sudden Infant Death Syndrome).

On the downside dummies are associated with several problems in babies and toddlers including:

- increased occurrence of middle-ear infections
- when used beyond six months there is impaired tooth, bite and mouth development
- speech delay if used too much during the daytime
- increased number of vomiting bugs, diarrhoea and fevers
- higher chance of colic.

Many parents therefore worry about dummy use and feel judged if their toddler uses a dummy. An over-reliance on dummies can reduce opportunities for your toddler to talk and also negatively affect the morphology of his teeth and jaw development. Ideally dummies should only be used in response to specific soothing needs in toddlers after 12 months; a dummy might still be used when your toddler is ill, hurts himself or goes to sleep but isn't permanently in his mouth all day.

Dummies can interfere with speech development in toddlers, so try to restrict their dummy time and make sure your toddler gets plenty of opportunities to talk, sing and listen during the day. If your toddler has a dummy in his mouth, explain that you cannot understand what he is saying and if he takes it out you can then more easily understand him. Toddlers get very frustrated when they can't be understood so this is a strong motivator to ditch the dummy during the daytime.

Weaning your toddler off a dummy

Is it hard to wean a toddler off a dummy? In a word, yes! Dummy-sucking and thumb-sucking (the latter I can personally attest to) are strong habits that can be very hard, upsetting and stressful to be weaned off. It can be so emotional that many parents wish they had never introduced a dummy in the first place, and avoid introducing a dummy with subsequent children.

Some parents find a 'coming of age' ceremony useful: this is where the toddler voluntarily hands over their dummies to a 'dummy fairy'. This can help a toddler or pre-schooler feel empowered to stop using one and in return he gets a thank-you present.

The dummy fairy ceremony might be a little too sophisticated for younger toddlers to cope with as it is quite a complicated and magical concept. Instead, it might be easier to slowly reduce the situations that your toddler is allowed to have his dummy in his mouth. If there's a time when you don't want your child to use a dummy, for example, when you are out and about, stick to your guns but try to side-track your child rather than be confrontational. A more gradual reduction in dummy use might make the transition easier for your toddler.

If you do go for gradual withdrawal from a dummy, it is easier for both you and your toddler if you have a rough plan in mind, so it's easy for you to be consistent and for your toddler to understand and accept the new rule. You may want to get to a point where your toddler is only using his dummy for naps and going to sleep. Rather than move straight to that point you could go for a few easier stages on the way:

- Stage 1: take your toddler's dummy out every time you speak to him and explain with, 'Mummy/Daddy can't hear what you say with your dummy in'
- Stage 2: no dummy at mealtimes or snacks. Explain each time with, 'Your mouth is eating now so no dummy so you can taste your food and grow strong'
- Stage 3: no dummy outside of the home. Explain that the dummy will be back at home for nap or bedtime but not when you are both out and about.

TOP TIP

Dummies can interfere with speech development in toddlers, so although you don't have to stop your child using one completely you really need to restrict their use. Make sure your toddler gets plenty of opportunity to talk and chat, and encourage no dummy or thumb-sucking during the daytime.

---

real parent story

Sharon (Arthur, 30 months)

'Arthur loved those big cherry dummies and got into the habit of having it in his mouth all the time. It was tough at night when he was little as he'd cry if he woke up and it had fallen out so I was forever going into his room, finding the dummy, and giving it back to him. In the end I'd put in about five in his bed at night (some were fluorescent) and he'd find them. During the day I wanted to prepare him for starting nursery when I went back to work, so about six months before, I started slowly reducing the time and situations he could have his dummy in. If he was sad I'd still get it out but eventually he just had it for naps and night-time which I was happy with.'

Thumb-sucking

Thumb-sucking shares some of the problems with prolonged dummy use in that it can affect the development of the teeth and jaw; thumbs can exert a stronger push on the back of the teeth and roof of the mouth than a dummy.

My youngest daughter was a thumb- sucker. She still sometimes puts her thumb in her mouth if I go to soothe her if she's hurt herself or is crying. Unlike dummies it's harder for parents to intervene as you can't take a thumb away from a child! However, I think partly because it takes some effort to hold a thumb in one's mouth and toddlers are always using their hands, you don't tend to see a toddler with their thumb in their mouth for hours on end (like you commonly see with dummies). Most thumb-suckers tend to grow out of the habit but in the meantime they can get infections and sore skin from having wet soggy skin. If you are worried about their teeth and skin infections, try and remind him to take his thumb out of his mouth during the day. I don't advocate painting mustard or bitter nail polishes onto the thumb. Speak to your dentist if you are concerned about your toddler's dental development and he or she will be able to advise if there is a problem.

Comfort blankets

Comforters, blankets, soft toys and other props are quite common for children to cuddle when they need reassurance. They can also be used as a 'magic talisman' when your toddler is tired, poorly, or has fallen over and grazed his knee. Comforters offer a powerful form of support to your developing toddler, although some toddlers never form a strong attachment to a soft toy or blanket. I had one toddler who never had a teddy or blanket. I quite missed having the prop to help him to settle if he was upset or I was leaving him with his Grandma, but otherwise there were no fundamental problems. He just wasn't a 'teddy boy'.

Toddlers who do love a soft toy or blanket can become very attached to their special comforter – as hundreds of parents learn to their woe when their toddler's beloved teddy gets lost or lands in a puddle and needs to go in the washing machine! Doctors and psychologists know the important role of these comforters, and when children are admitted to hospital it is one of the facts that is recorded about the child – so all staff know the name and description of the little patient's comforter.

As children develop emotionally they become increasingly aware that they are an individual and that their parents sometimes are not with them to comfort them. Being able to receive comfort from cuddling a teddy or blanket is a powerful milestone in your toddler's development as he becomes able to use a comforter as a way of 'self-soothing'. A soother can be such a powerful trigger of sleep that some toddlers will instinctively yawn and snuggle when handed their comforter or toy. When your toddler comes into light sleep, if the comforter is with him he may begin to use the comforter to touch base and then return to sleep. All human beings wake during the night between 90-minute sleep cycles, and we learn to go back to sleep. Using a comforter can mean he is less likely to need you to soothe him back to sleep, and may drop off more quickly when he wakes in the night.

Comforters are a great prop in your toddler's toolkit. They help him cope with uncertainty, anxiety, pain, fear and other emotions. For this reason I would recommend trying to offer your toddler a comforter or appropriate soft toy, although some toddlers (like my son) will not want one.

One of the drawbacks is that if a child becomes upset when he cannot find or have his comforter he can become more distressed than by the incident which precipitated needing the comforter.

Try not to worry about your child being devoted to a teddy or a blanket as it isn't a 'bad habit'. Comforters are very common and most children tend to slowly reduce the time they rely on their comforter as they get older.

As long as constantly holding the teddy or blanket isn't stopping him from playing and leading a happy, energetic life I wouldn't worry too much. I don't think there should ever come a time when a loved teddy bear should be consigned to the bin.

What tends to happen is that as a child gets older and more self-conscious he might choose to put the comforter away or even get rid of it. I still have my teddy Panda Woo Woo, but now my children play with him.

Taking comforters to childcare

Most nurseries are sensitive to a toddler's need to bring their comforter to nursery, especially when settling in. This is an example of a toddler using a prop to help support his internal emotional resources to manage a situation – and this should be encouraged. When your toddler is able to use a comforter when you are not there it is one of the first examples of emotional self-regulation. It can be a stepping-stone to help your toddler cope with fears and anxieties that he might face each day.

In time, the comforter can be left in the 'precious box' or in a bag on your child's peg for special situations like a grazed knee. Quite soon many children are happy to wait until they get home to cuddle their teddy.

As a parent you can use similar tactics if you are out and about. Instead of taking the comforter everywhere (where it can be easily lost) it can instead travel in the car or under the pram so your toddler isn't constantly carrying it around. Parents need to be sensitive to their child's needs and judge how best to manage this, and not be motivated by their own fear of judgement by other adults.

SIXTEEN RABBITS ON THE WASHING LINE

I have three children but only one of them, Miranda, fell deeply in love with a soft toy. It was a white rabbit and she loved to suck its long towelling ears when she was tired, sad and poorly.

Very early on, when she seemed to have singled out the 'Baddit', I bought a couple of duplicates in case we ever lost the Baddit … and we did. We left them at various locations around the country (grandparents, Botanical Gardens, supermarket) and thanked our lucky stars that we had back-ups.

When Miranda was nine months old she developed a rare immune disorder which meant she attacked and wiped out her own white blood cells. The illness meant two things: first she was in hospital frequently suffering the pain of having cannulas fitted to give her IV antibiotics; and second, she had virtually no resistance to bacterial infections.

The hospital put down 'Baddit' in her medical notes as a 'spiritual aid'. This meant we needed more Baddits so we could keep them super-clean and have them on hand to soothe her through her illness.

At one time we had 16 Baddits! She didn't seem to mind the fact that she had so many versions, and as an attachment specialist I did used to wonder when she would ask for a 'fresh bunny', and if she would have a similarly disposable attitude to boyfriends in the future!

Miranda recovered from her illness at the age of three and is no longer a Baddit Addict but we still have about six Baddits left.

I think that her comforters really supported her through her tough illness and I have such fond memories of all those 'Baddits' drying on the washing line.

TOP TIP

As soon as your toddler or baby falls in love with a particular comforter soft toy you could get several versions so they can be rotated; this way your toddler is not bereft if the comforter gets lost or needs washing.

chapter seventeen

potty learning

'Rules governing defecation, hygiene, and pollution exist in every culture at every period in history. It may, in fact, be the foundation of civilization: What is toilet training if not the first attempt to turn a child into an acceptable member of society?'

Rose George

It can sometimes seem that your entire role as a parent hinges on when your toddler is potty-trained. When babies in the UK were all wearing towelling nappies with big nappy pins and water-proof pants there was a big cultural and personal imperative for earlier potty training. Having to clean, 'bleach', wash and dry up to ten nappies a day was a huge motivator!

I have chosen to call this chapter potty 'learning' rather than potty 'training', as this approach highlights your toddler's natural ability and motivation to develop self-care, as opposed to the idea of the parent 'breaking in' and training their toddler like a lion tamer.

The disposable nappies available today are so absorbent that fewer nappies are used each day, and using nappies can seem more convenient and easy than moving to underpants and the need to have a loo or a potty close by. However, with the environmental considerations and the expectations of grandparents and peers, there is social pressure on parents to potty train as early as possible. According to the University of Michigan, the physical skills needed for successful potty learning appear between 18 and 30 months in girls and boys.[1] The average age for girls to be potty-trained is

---

1 Blum N.J., Taubman B., Nemeth N., 'Relationship between age at initiation of toilet training and duration of training: a prospective study (*Pediatrics* 2003 Apr; 111: 810–4)

29 months, and the average age for boys is 31 months. There is a large range in the actual age that toddlers can be categorically described as fully potty-trained, but nearly all (98 per cent) children are fully potty-trained by their third birthday.

Physiological development

Trends and nappy equipment may have changed over the years, but what has not changed are toddlers' bodies. The stages of physiological development of potty learning begin with involuntary (or incontinent) pooing and weeing that all babies demonstrate with flair.

Over time there is a transition to increased voluntary control of the bladder, bowel and sphincters. This is, and has always been, a process. First, you will observe a pattern between when your baby or toddler has a feed and when she has a poo. Eating stimulates peristalsis (the involuntary muscle rhythms that push waste products down to the rectum and out through the anus) so that all the involuntary smooth muscles of the gut push food down the gut where nutrients are absorbed and then water is removed and waste products are added. If your toddler's gut is working effectively, and her diet is balanced (with plenty of fibre, fruits and vegetables) you will notice that soon after a meal she will need a poo.

There is a difference between the reflex to empty the bladder or rectum, and the voluntary expulsion of these waste products, though they often get combined.

You will first notice that your toddler's body times weeing and pooing after eating, about five minutes after a meal. This is largely a reflex driven by involuntary muscle control such as peristalsis in the gut. You can use this timing pattern to help your toddler associate weeing and pooing with being on the potty. It's a matter of being in the right place at the right time.

At around 18 months of age you may see that the timing reflex isn't as strong as your toddler exerts increasing voluntary control over her body. This can lead to constipation and impaction so is not hugely helpful during potty learning. It's hard to know why toddlers sometimes hold in poos, but it led Sigmund Freud to formulate complicated theories of people he termed as 'anal-retentives' and 'anal-expulsives'. I think toddlers sometimes hold in a poo if they are side-tracked and don't want to stop playing. Your toddler might also begin to hold in poo if she's had a painful experience and become scared of pooing. In this situation it's important to make sure your toddler's poo is soft and easy to pass. Lots of fruit and sweetcorn can help and in extreme cases your doctor my prescribe a stool softener such as Lactulose to help them pass stools without pain. This helps them to lose their fear of pooing.

Signs of readiness to potty learn

Here are some signs, physical, behavioural and cognitive, that your toddler is ready to start potty learning:

Physical signs

Your toddler needs to have the physical ability to use the potty or loo, including being able to balance on it!

- stays dry for over two hours during the day. This can be quite hard to assess if your toddler is wearing a highly absorbent nappy
- has a dry nappy after a nap or when she wakes up in the morning
- poos at a predictable time (e.g. after breakfast) each day
- no poos overnight
- does big, long wees, meaning a full bladder is being emptied rather than continual incontinence. You may notice this if your toddler's nappy doesn't need changing for a while during the day, and then it's suddenly very full and heavy
- being able to comfortably get onto, and sit on, the potty or loo.

Behavioural signs

There may be some clues that your toddler is ready to use the potty or loo. She might enjoy this new move to becoming independent.

- able to pull up and down trousers or skirt
- asks to be changed or tries to remove dirty nappies because they are uncomfortable
- tells you she needs to wee or poo or signals when she is pooing or weeing
- keen to stop wearing a nappy in favour of knickers or underpants
- keen to sit on a potty
- keen to be a 'big' girl or boy
- likes being cooperative
- not afraid or resistant to the potty or loo
- says 'I do it' a lot, and craves independence
- takes pride in independence and new skills.

Cognitive signs

Your toddler needs to have the words or signs to be able to communicate when she needs the loo.

- anticipates needing the loo with an initially urgent sense that pooing or weeing is about to happen. She will only get a few seconds warning at first, so you need to have a potty to hand very quickly
- may have words for poo, wee, potty, nappy
- is able to and keen to follow simple instructions
- understands the physical signals that mean she has to go, and can tell you before it happens, or even hold it until she has time to get to the potty.

Toddler-led potty learning

Potty training or learning tends to go more smoothly if it is toddler-led and toddler-desired. However, you will still need to line up your ducks and have a plan of action to facilitate your toddler's potty learning. Try to time introducing the potty at a time when things are most relaxed at home. Times to avoid are: around the birth of a new baby, an older sibling starting school, moving home, and around times of lots of travelling and visiting, for example, the Christmas holidays.

First, be sure that your toddler is ready (see points above).

Second, choose the equipment you will need for your toddler. I recommend:

- a double loo seat that gives toddlers the option of going straight onto the big loo, but with a smaller seat that comes down to make her feel secure. This can be a better option for tall toddlers who can find potties placed on the floor uncomfortable to balance on
- a home potty at home. I found the high-backed potties with a removable potty compartment have been preferred by my toddlers as they could sit more comfortably on it
- a travel potty. I found a fold-up travel potty, kept under the pram, was a real bonus for those days when I had to be out and about with my toddlers, and they could only give me a short 'warning' that they needed to go
- lots of underpants. You could choose some appealing 'big' boy or girl pants with your toddler (I also used hand-me-downs from cousins as back-up). I don't really recommend those 'big kid' style low-absorbent 'pull-ups' for potty learning, as they are neither one thing (an absorbent nappy) or another (a grown-up pair of knickers). Although the full-absorbent pull-up nappies can be useful before potty learning with a walking toddler as they are easier to put on and take off. (They might also be useful if you have an older

toddler who is struggling with potty learning but doesn't want to wear a 'baby nappy'. You will know best what underwear will be most appropriate for your toddler)

- *Everybody Poos,* by Taro Gomi, really helped my youngest (and slowest potty learner) to feel comfortable with the whole fact she pooed waste that needed to be flushed away
- a spare set of clothes for on the go and lots to hand in the home.

Third, plan to set aside at least a week to do some potty learning at home. This means waiting for a school holiday or half term if you have older siblings who go to school or preschool each day so you have time to focus. When you are ready to start, here are my tips to help you both:

1. Keep your toddler very well-hydrated, and give her a diet full of fruits and vegetables to make pooing easy and frequent; these foods include apricots, beetroots and sweetcorn.
2. Let your toddler get used to sitting on the new potty and/or toddler loo seat.
3. If possible, have a 'bare bum' home week. This is easier in summer, especially if you have a garden.
4. After a big wee and poo let your toddler try on her first pair of big girl pants.
5. Explain that when these pants get wet or dirty they will feel uncomfortable, so your toddler and you will work as a team to give a signal and get to the potty.
6. After breakfast (or whenever your toddler tends to have a poo), ask her to sit on the potty and read a story or have a chat while she waits for something to happen.
7. Give your child lots of big drinks and say, 'Let's see if your next wee can be on the potty.'
8. If your toddler wees or poos in the new pants be completely relaxed about it. Say, 'Oh, you've done a wee/poo in your pants; that must feel uncomfortable. Never mind, let's get you changed and next time let's work as a team to get to the potty.'

TOP TIP

In the early days of potty learning the idea is to let your toddler notice the signs that she needs a wee or a poo. Getting to the potty on time, along with your praise, is reward in itself so don't feel that you need to give a treat each time she manages this.

TOP TIP

Try to use phrases that specifically highlight the benefits of what she has achieved, e.g., 'You must feel like such a big girl wearing your new pants', or, 'I bet you feel proud to sit on the big loo like mummy does and do a wee!'

What if my toddler regresses?

Even with everything set up well for potty learning, things can set your toddler back. Illness or a developmental leap in another area can mean that your toddler isn't motivated or able to perfect this new major skill simultaneously. Bad experiences of potty learning can also lead to a reluctance; constipation or an anal fissure can lead to painful pooing, and the pain sets up an association and can lead to a phobia of the potty.

In this case it's better to relax, take a break, and come back to potty learning after a week or a few days. Try not to make it into a huge deal as this can lead to a stubborn toddler digging in her heels, or an anxious toddler getting increasingly stressed around the potty. Try to avoid the use of laxatives, although your doctor may suggest a stool softener like Lactulose to get through a period of fear and pain if your toddler has an anal fissure.

TOP TIP

In the case of constipation or a bad experience, it's really important to get your toddler's gut moving so that lots of easy pooing happens. Try to include lots of gut-regulating food such as water, beetroot, apricots, figs and sweetcorn. You might also want to reduce the amount of food that might exacerbate constipation, such as cheese and red meat, for a while. Lots of exercise can help too.

The 'elimination communication' method

Elimination communication, also known as 'infant potty training' and 'nappy-free', is a new phrase for a parenting technique that has been used in nappy-free societies for millennia.

In countries like China, infants wear crotchless pants or trousers and their parents aim to learn to recognise the signs that their baby is about to poo and wee, for example, a suddenly puce face. They hold the baby while he or she wees or poos. It is more straightforward in warm countries as there are no shopping centres, restaurants or shagpile carpets; babies can simply be held away by their carer until she's finished weeing and pooing straight onto the ground.

Other solutions have been developed around the world, including hoods filled with arctic moss for Inuit babies, and Asian cradles called *beshiks*, with a hole for excretions to come out of the cradle.

In the West, elimination communication is associated with an 'attachment' parenting style, where parents get used to the signals their baby gives for hunger, tiredness and pooing and then respond. The aim of parents using elimination communication is twofold: to tap into a baby's signals that she needs to poo or wee and respond. Second, to reduce or remove the need for nappies. If you read any of the forums on the subject, there is a wide range of experience. Some parents report that it happens really easily, with others reporting that they find the technique hard work and their toddler hasn't potty trained earlier than their peers in nappies.

Elimination communication is a form of behavioural conditioning, where an association between feeling pooing or weeing happening is inextricably linked with sitting on a potty. Some toddlers are less easily conditioned than others; their brains simply don't make the association as easily. This will explain some of the range in success of this technique from child to child with some parents reporting successes from six to nine months of age.

As with all options for looking after your toddler I would encourage you to think what will work for you, and try not to feel pressurised by what other people recommend.

I expect that elimination communication would best suit parents who are committed to green living, who are 'stay at home' and literally have a 'go with the flow' attitude. I doubt many nurseries would offer elimination communication support as one of their services.

Although I have never used the technique, I imagine it would require a very child-centred and patient attitude. One of the parents I knew that used the elimination communication potty training schedule, realised that it did not suit her. The family had an immaculate home for a start, and the parents often got frustrated if the toddler had an 'accident' (for want of a better word). Their whole world, at the time, seemed to be orbiting around potty training and the toddler began holding in poos. Now, that said, the family may have had a similarly miserable time whatever the technique used, but this case highlights the need for parents to think about the reality of their lives. Too often parents feel pressurised to follow a certain parenting expert or technique when the advice just doesn't suit their temperament, priorities or lifestyle.

Many parents who have success with this method report that they go through fewer (rather than none) nappies. It might be unrealistic to expect that all babies will respond perfectly to the system, but it might have some benefit to better understanding your baby's timing, which may help her be nappy- and accident-free before she reaches toddlerhood.

Night-time dryness

This is not something you can force to happen and it is often completely unrelated to a toddler's progress with daytime weeing and pooing on the potty. Whilst most toddlers no longer poo in the night, there is a big range in bedwetting.

Some toddlers are dry through the night at quite a young age and some toddlers aren't. Studies around the world have consistently reported one in five five-year-olds display bedwetting. At this age it is referred to as primary nocturnal enuresis (PNE) and is more common in boys. This means that these children do not have consistently dry nights. One of my friend's sons was still wetting the bed fairly frequently at the age of seven years. He had potty trained really early, but he displayed many of the factors shared by other older children who experience PNE. This includes drinking a lot during the day and sleeping very deeply.

You should not have high expectations about when your toddler will be dry at night. Night-time dryness seems to be largely governed by vasopressin, which is a hormone that regulates urination (our internal diuretic). There is a big range in physiology, sleeping behaviour and temperament amongst toddlers. There is nothing you can do in terms of 'disciplining' a bedwetter; it wouldn't work, it would be cruel, and it would be counterproductive ... bedwetting can actually be brought on by severe stress.

TOP TIP

You may find that your child who has been dry at night for months wets the bed in anticipation of starting preschool or after a stressful event. You will need to take these events in your stride and reassure your child that she hasn't done anything wrong and sometimes our bodies react when we are upset. It's important to reassure your child about the underlying stress too.

It's best to be patient and wait until your toddler is consistently dry before you ditch the night-time nappies. Avoid giving her lots of fluids last thing at night. When your child has had lots of dry nights in a row you might want to stop using nappies at night. Also include the following steps:

- offer your a toddler a wee last thing at night
- place an undersheet bed mat on your toddler's bed to protect the mattress from a wee
- have a potty in her room and a night light if she would like that security and to be able to find the potty easily
- leave a night light on near the bathroom for night-time trips
- some children who wet the bed after they have started school can sometimes benefit from being taken for a 'sleepy wee' before you go to bed at around 10pm, but I wouldn't recommend waking up your toddler to try and have a dry night.

Potty learning dilemmas

Q: What if my toddler refuses to let me flush away the contents of the potty?

A: This was something that my youngest toddler did and is a fairly common reaction for many toddlers. They feel like they are losing a part of themselves (it did come out of their body after all), and they feel protective and almost panicky when it disappears. Try to be patient and explain the basic biology to them – this is the leftover food that your body doesn't need any more. Don't insist that she flushes it away until she shows an interest herself. My eldest daughter drew a cartoon which she stuck next to both of our loos. It showed a shoal of fish in the sea thanking her for the scrummy lunch. Now, I'm not advocating this attitude to sewage pollution at all, but it reassured my toddler, and after a few days of unflushed loos she was able to flush away her poos and wees herself.

Q: I have to take my toddler on a long car journey. Can I put him back in a nappy for the trip so he doesn't have an accident?

A: It's not a good idea to change back to nappies once you and your toddler are potty learning. I would suggest postponing potty training until after a long drive, say to go on holiday. If you have no choice, perhaps avoid the motorways and instead build in lots of time for lots of stops. It was actually a rather wonderful way to travel which I would recommend in general for small children. To them (unless they are blissfully asleep) they see the journey as part of the holiday or the trip and it's possible to really go slow and enjoy it too. It can be a good idea to put a towel under your toddler's bottom in the car (with a couple of spares) so that if she does wee in her sleep or has an accident, you can keep her car seat clean and dry and simply pull over and change her.

Q: My toddler says she wants her nappies back.

A: You need to look at the back story to this request. If your toddler has been having lots of accidents and feels a bit defeated, she might not yet be ready, so you could go back to nappies and try again in a week or so. Potty learning can often be more of a two steps forwards and one step backward path, so don't feel like you have failed if this has happened.

However, if you feel like your toddler is nearly there you could let her choose some new underpants or knickers. She will be excited to choose her own pack, which will be more interesting than her nappies, and it might give her the impetus she needs to move away from nappies for good.

Q: My toddler likes to sit down and pee on the potty but he won't poo there.

A: This is very common, so try not to get too anxious; pooing is more physically demanding than weeing. If your toddler needs a wee, then one little muscular push and the wee will flow. Pooing can be much harder work and if the potty is unstable, or the loo is very high, your toddler can feel vulnerable and unsteady as he has to make a concerted effort to push out the poo over several minutes. Toddlers often stand up to poo in their nappy and this is actually easier than sitting down if the potty or toilet is at the wrong height. It's a bit like active birthing – allowing gravity and your muscles to effectively bear down make both birth of a baby and pushing out a poo easier! This added concentration and difficulty can really put off toddlers pooing. One thing to make things easier is to make sure that your toddler has an efficient gut with soft poo (see page 194).

Q: My toddler is starting nursery and I'm worried about how she will get on.

A: It can be very stressful for a parent if you feel under pressure for your toddler to be potty-trained before she starts nursery. However, accidents are fairly common even at preschool and most nurseries are used to dealing with a range of potty learning stages. Nurseries offering care to younger toddlers will change nappies as a matter of course.

Q: My toddler has the occasional accident. How should I respond?

A: It's really important not to get angry or shame your toddler if she has an accident, even if you feel tired and frustrated. Instead, let your toddler know that accidents happen. Don't dwell on the past (as she can't go back in time and undo the accident) and say: 'Don't worry, accidents happen sometimes, and we can try next time to get to the potty.' It's not a good idea to make your toddler clear up an accident as punishment as this may stress and shame your toddler.

real parent story

Sarah, parent to Josh (5 years)

'Josh has always been a deep sleeper, I'm not sure if that's anything to do with it but he still wets the bed frequently and he's nearly six. I've tried to reduce his liquid intake in the evening and woken him up when we go to bed for a sleepy wee but I'm hoping he'll grow out of it as I'm fed up of washing his top sheet all the time and I want him to be able to go to Beaver's camp and sleepovers without wetting the bed.'

Take this potty learning quiz to see if your toddler is ready to learn to use a potty.

Quiz: Is your toddler ready to start potty learning?

These questions look at the physical, cognitive and emotional readiness of your toddler. She will also need to have the communication skills needed to begin potty learning. It can also show you how ready you and the household are to start potty learning.

1. When my toddler has a poo in her nappy she has a recognisable pose:
   a) Not really.
   b) Sometimes.
   c) She strikes a pose that I can recognise at 100 paces and often goes somewhere quiet to poo.

2. My toddler has a poo at set times of day, e.g. after breakfast:
   a) There is no pattern to her pooing.
   b) Sometimes there seems to be a pattern but it changes all the time.
   c) You could set a watch to her poos.

3. My toddler has a wet nappy that needs changing:
   a) Frequently, with lots of little wees every one or two hours.
   b) Fairly frequently with some very wet nappies and some lightly wet nappies.
   c) She seems to save up her wees for one big wee every two to three hours.

4. My toddler is interested in self-care and understands phrases and words like 'done poo?', 'wet' and 'dry':
   a) Not really.
   b) She seems to understand some of these words and concepts but doesn't say them.
   c) She talks with me about pooing and weeing.

5. How does your toddler let you know she has an urge to wee or poo?
   a) She doesn't but sometimes I recognise her behaviour.
   b) She tells me 'go away' or 'poo poo'.
   c) She fully describes when she's pooing and weeing.

6. What stage are your toddler's physical motor skills at?
   a) She struggles to climb on and off furniture or sit on a chair.
   b) With a bit of help she can climb on and off furniture and sit with balance.
   c) She already climbs and sits on the potty and loo.

7. Can your toddler undress herself?
   a) She's just started with pulling off her socks.
   b) With a bit of help.
   c) She can pull down her trousers properly.

8. How does your toddler respond to directions?
   a) She doesn't yet understand one-word directions, e.g. 'give' and 'stop'.
   b) Will follow very simple instructions, e.g. 'come here'.
   c) Understands two-stage instructions, e.g. 'pick up the block and give it to me'.

9. How independent is your toddler?
   a) She's still happy for me to help her with most things.
   b) She occasionally wants to do things herself.
   c) 'Me do it!' is her favourite phrase.

10. Do you have any upheavals on the horizon?
    a) We are moving soon in time for the new baby.
    b) It's quite hectic at the minute.
    c) Our days are quiet and predictable at the moment.

You will need to weigh up all the answers but overall if you answered:

Mostly As: Your toddler may really struggle to learn to use the potty right now.

Mostly Bs: Your toddler is starting to have the skills needed to successfully learn to use the potty. You may like to try a comfortable potty or loo seat to see how interested she is. Find a nice book about potties at the library, and see how engaged she is in the idea.

Mostly Cs: Your toddler has most of the skills she needs to learn to use the potty, so if the time is right for you too, you could start!

food and eating

'They say fingers were made before forks and hands before knives.'

Jonathan Swift

There is so much going on in the toddler years when it comes to food. Your toddler will be learning about new tastes and textures, moving to three meals a day, will be eating more at the table with the family and will be learning to feed himself. There is a lot going on. And that's even before he starts to have an opinion on what he does and doesn't like!

Why can toddlers get choosy about food?

On the whole toddlers prefer sweet-tasting or high-calorie foods; this reflects a human instinct born back in the Palaeolithic era when obesity was unheard of and the preference for high-calorie food was beneficial and a good strategy for our hunter-gatherer ancestors. This means that a toddler, given his own choice, might happily eat biscuits day in, day out, or indeed any food that just fills his stomach. It falls to you to offer instead a balanced diet of food, flavours and textures to educate his palate. This means a range of:

- good fats: e.g. avocado, coconut oil and foods containing omega 3 fatty oils such as seeds and oily fish)
- dairy: e.g. eggs, full-fat milk, cheese and natural yoghurt
- carbohydrates: e.g. potatoes, rice, pasta and bread

- protein: e.g. red meat, white meat, fish, lentils and pulses
- fruit and vegetables: aim for lots of vegetables and fruits each day. Fruit juice isn't recommended as you don't get the useful fibre with it as you do with fruit.

When toddlers turn their nose up at a new food (neophobia) it may partly be due to our evolutionary past. Being cautious of new food could protect them from eating poison, although this behaviour is very contrary as it seems to fail toddlers at crucial moments, such as when they come across new poisonous berries or brightly coloured dishwasher tablets!

TOP TIP

In general, many low-fat 'diet' foods and high-fibre foods are inappropriate for toddlers. Diet foods are often full of sugar to replace the flavour of the fat with sweetness. Perhaps surprisingly, eating wholegrain or brown versions of bread and rice is not recommended until your toddler is two or above as it is more difficult to absorb calories from wholemeal foods.

Sharing meals as a family

One major way that children learn is by 'modelling' or copying older and more experienced people. By watching you pick up a spear of asparagus and bite off the end or dip a toast soldier into a boiled egg, your toddler will absorb, watch and learn unconsciously. With the use of their mirror neurons (see page 250), his brain will mentally 'rehearse' new physical skills as he watches his proficient elders.

In order to develop the myriad physical skills required to feed themselves, children flourish in a relaxed environment where their physical dexterity with knives, forks, spoons, chopsticks and hands improves. These gross and fine motor skills will seem normal and important to your toddler as he shares a meal with his family. If every time he eats, he is sitting alone and ignored in a highchair, he loses the rich and loving environment that helps him to learn to love and respect food.

You will also be able to slowly and warmly introduce manners that you and your family think are important at the table. Your idea of table manners may be to ask the person next to you if they would like more water before you refill you own glass. Children pick up on these habits and the behaviour you would like to see at the table needs to be modelled by you, preferably during lots of relaxed and warm family meals.

TOP TIP

The old saying: 'The family that eats together, stays together' might seem trite but I do think that sitting with your toddler and talking to him at mealtimes is really valuable. Ideally, try to eat with your toddler so that you model good eating habits and a warm and positive attitude to food.

It's a mistake to see your toddler's meals as a time to check Facebook. I know this is easier said than done when you want to relax after a hectic morning or afternoon but it will pay dividends.

When your baby is first starting to eat solids and starting to eat three meals a day, it is perhaps not realistic that you will be able to share each meal with him as you may be helping him a lot with his food (and he will eat slowly). However, as he becomes a toddler and moves to three meals a day, try to stop, slow down and just sit and chat to him while he eats. Not only is it important that he is supervised if he's eating in case he chokes, but it becomes a good habit for both of you.

If you can't manage it all the time, make a promise to yourself that you will all have your Sunday lunch together around a table. A family table is a vital bit of equipment and if your toddler is using a highchair bring it to the table too.

> **TOP TIP**
>
> Sharing meals is about so much more than just eating and taking in 'fuel'. Sharing food, whether in cultural and religious feasts like Passover or Christmas Day or simply Sunday lunch around the table, is a deeply important opportunity for your toddler's social, emotional and physical development. Your toddler will learn so much and benefit deeply from sharing meals with you, his siblings, and the extended family and community.

Hunger and fullness

In my experience, a toddler that has been allowed to develop his own appetite and satiety instincts will quickly feel full with high-calorie food and will not eat it to excess. Parents seem to vacillate between worrying that their toddler prefers bad food, and worrying that they don't eat enough. Don't worry that your toddler will starve; like cats they are very good at regulating their appetite, as long as you are offering regular, balanced and nutritious meals and snacks.

Your toddler's appetite and satiety skills need to be supported from birth, whether breastfeeding or formula feeding. From birth, babies display feeding cues of hunger (rooting for the breasts, licking lips and eventually crying). They also have feeding cues for fullness (closing their mouth, turning their head away, fussing and spitting out milk or food). It is really important for your toddler to learn to self-regulate his appetite. This means while it is important to offer him a big range of foods, don't force him to eat things or finish everything on his plate. It forces him to ignore the fullness messages from his brain, and he could lose the important ability to eat mindfully, to eat when hungry and stop when full. The Department of Health states (in their leaflets to healthcare professionals) that there are no set portion sizes for toddlers and don't recommend that children should be forced to finish meals. This is because they are concerned that this approach may pave the way for childhood obesity.

> **TOP TIP**
>
> Use toddler-sized plates and bowls so as not to overwhelm them.

Is your toddler a super-taster?

Being a 'super-taster' isn't some kind of super power. It is a name that describes around one quarter of adults and children who have a strong sensitivity to taste, especially bitter tastes. The tongues of super-tasters have more tastebuds and they often find foods with some bitter flavours unpalatable, e.g. sprouts and broccoli can taste delicious to many of us but really unbearable to super-tasters. They are also more sensitive to sugar, sour flavours and rich creamy food. Girls and women are more likely to be super-tasters as are people with African, Asian and South American heritage.

Of the rest of the population, half are considered medium-tasters, leaving another quarter at the other end of the scale – they are the so-called 'non-tasters'. Super-tasting is genetically inherited, and is due to a higher density and number of tastebuds on the tongue which perceive flavour and taste. Super-tasters display less enjoyment of fatty and sugary foods but more of a preference for salty foods. As a group they tend to weigh less than others.

To test whether or not someone is a super-taster depends on their sensitivity to a bitter compound called 6-n-propylthiouracil (PROP). Non-tasters can't actually taste the bitterness of

PROP, medium-tasters don't mind PROP but can taste it, while super-tasters find the taste of PROP horrible.

As you may have guessed, toddlers taste PROP more strongly than adults and (unlike adults), children always taste the bitterness of PROP. This probably means that certain foods taste different to your toddler than they do to you. This might be the crux of the 'picky toddler' syndrome

If your toddler is an extreme super-taster, he will find bitter compounds found in vegetables really unpleasant and may not 'eat his greens'. The good news is that if your toddler is a super-taster he will be sated with less sugar and fat, but on the downside, super-tasters often avoid really nutritious dark green vegetables and crave more salt.

It should be noted that without a proper test (which are available for adults to buy on the internet), you shouldn't just assume that your toddler is a super-taster if he turns his nose up at certain foods. However, if you begin to see strong aversions to particularly bitter foods you may need to offer less bitter vegetables such as mangetout or fresh peas alongside the more bitter veggies such as broccoli. It could help to avoid a few upset lunchtimes until your child's tastes mature.

Is sugar bad for your toddler?

Too many empty calories from refined sugar (such as from sweets, biscuits, sugary breakfast cereals and fizzy drinks) will lead to sugar 'crashes'; this is where your toddler's blood sugar will crash after a sweet food, which can lead to feelings of moodiness, anger and increased tantrums. I'm not a proponent of a 'zero sugar' approach, as it can go hand-in-hand with zero fun. Baking as a family or eating birthday cake at a party is good fun and labelling some foods as 'bad' can cause its own problems. I think a 'zero sugar approach' can lead to an overly anxious, obsessive and puritanical attitude to food which parents can unwittingly pass on to their child.

Coeliac disease

If you are really concerned about your toddler's diet or growth, speak to your health visitor or GP and get your toddler weighed and measured. This is particularly important if you have noticed that your toddler is having any digestion problems such as bloating, diarrhoea, constipation, pale poo covered in mucus, or he says he has tummy ache after eating as these could be linked to coeliac disease. A recent study found that doctors were able to predict coeliac disease (an autoimmune disease that affects 1 in 100 people) in 80 per cent of toddlers and young children simply by looking for low growth rates amongst children. My elder daughter was diagnosed with coeliac disease with a blood test when she was six. She had no tummy ache but her growth had dropped off and she was permanently like a person suffering with low blood sugar: tired, grumpy and emotional. She began to crave high-sugar food. Her doctor explained that her gut was damaged and was not absorbing nutrients, so she craved food that was easy to digest and gave instant energy. The transformation in her mood and happiness when she went onto a gluten-free diet was wonderful.

Learning to feed himself

The gross and fine motor control required to scoop food onto a spoon, put to the mouth, and eat the food off the spoon is difficult, and may not develop until after 18 months. Finger foods make early self-feeding much easier. Even as your child enters toddlerhood he will still be learning about, and experimenting with lots of different textures, shapes and tastes.

Soft finger foods, like grated cheese and the whites of hard-boiled eggs, really help to develop your toddler's tastebuds, and the ability to cope with, and enjoy, new foods. Offer foods that can be picked up in a pincer grip (between finger and opposable thumb), such as sweetcorn and peas.

If your toddler is eating something with a runny consistency, such as homemade soup, you can let him have his own spoon or let him dip toast soldiers in it. You can also spear soft foods like cooked carrot onto a fork and let him practise bringing the fork to his mouth; don't be disheartened if he prefers to use his fingers. All these eating skills and tasting experiences are valuable, and hands are the easiest 'utensils' for your baby to use! Try to keep calm and relaxed around mealtimes and your toddler will feel the same, and will enjoy his new steps towards independence

What should I do if my toddler throws his food?

Parents, and especially some grandparents with rose-tinted memories of the past, can have unrealistic expectations about a toddler's dexterity and table manners. If you would like calm, happy mealtimes, then knowing what is truly possible for your child will help. Don't make mealtimes a battleground. When a toddler drops food, squashes it, and generally makes a mess, he is not being naughty. Toddlers may throw food to get a reaction out of you, especially if you are absorbed with your smartphone and ignoring him! So try not to react if he drops or throws food as he may like to repeat it. Make sure you chat to him so he gets plenty of attention and praise.

To make things easier for you, add a wipe clean cloth under your toddler's highchair so cleaning up is easy. The more calm and relaxed you can be, the more relaxed he will be.

How do you communicate about food?

Toddlers rely on the 'social referencing' of their family to understand everything, including food. Facial expressions are key in all this. In our evolutionary past, if a parent was disgusted as she or he tasted a new berry and spat it out it was helpful that a child watched and learned. The facial expression of disgust is so power-ful that toddlers don't need language to understand it, so bear in mind what you and your face communicate about food. Try to be positive, open and adventurous in your own eating behaviour to allow your toddler to model your positive behaviour.

Food should be a joy and an adventure and we should be keen to try a wide range of food and enjoy a healthy diet. Try to avoid passing on any personal hang-ups and prejudice about food; your toddler might love mushrooms even if you don't!

Grow your own

It is vital to develop a real love and understanding of the food we eat. Toddlers are more interested in food when they get to take part in the sowing, growing, harvesting and cooking of it. This is especially important if your child is choosy about what he eats; try to get him as involved in the growing, choosing and preparation as possible, rather than just present him with some-thing he had no part in.

For millennia, humans have hunted, gathered and grown our own food. Even our grandparents learned about where food came from when they were children, how to prepare food, and how to cook it. It was a *huge* part of their learning. During the WWII 'Dig for Victory' campaign there were nearly 1.5 million allotments in Britain but this has shrunk to fewer than 300,000 allotments now despite a huge demand from families for space to grow their own food. The good news is that you only need a bit of space in the garden or on a sunny windowsill to allow you and your toddler to have some meditative and calming garden-ing and growing time.

Our meat is packaged into cellophane-covered squares and our food is often delivered to our home pre-prepared or frozen. However, that doesn't mean that it is impossible for our toddlers to begin to understand what food is and how it is grown and cooked. I am not advocating a return to milling our own grains and living a subsistence farming lifestyle like *The Good Life*, but shopping at the market, growing a few herbs and visiting a 'pick-your-own' can all help.

If you eat seasonally your toddler will begin to understand that different foods grow at different times of the year. Even with just a windowsill you can teach your toddler about growing plants that he can eat. Simple things to grow include:

- cress in a pot on a damp piece of cotton wool
- mint, parsley and basil can be used during meals and your toddler will love being allowed to rip off a few leaves to sprinkle on everyone's meal
- salad leaves, or you can buy a tray of salad leaves that your toddler will enjoy harvesting to put on everyone's plate
- a potted strawberry or blueberry plant is an easy fruit to pick and a joy to eat.

TOP TIP

Growing food is a real test of 'delayed gratification' where a toddler begins to understand that he has to nurture and wait for the prize ... the harvest. Your toddler will be really excited with his first berries or carrots, and he might even present you with one!

Cooking with your toddler

Although toddler cooking and baking is not for the faint-hearted toddlers enjoy stirring, spooning, sieving and sprinkling. He can have a go at buttering toast, cutting soft cheese with a blunt child's knife, and can pull grapes off a bunch (though he will still need spherical foods cut up for him).

The earlier you can teach your toddler about the pleasure of cooking and preparing healthy food, the more confident he will feel about vital cooking skills (that mean he won't need to buy ready meals cooked in industrial quantities). If you feel that you know nothing about food and cooking, try to learn alongside your toddler with easy to prepare meals such as baked potatoes and omelettes to provide you both with nutritious food.

Eating dilemmas

Q: What should I do if my toddler doesn't want to eat his lunch?

A: It's important not to communicate, in your words and your behaviour, that you are anxious or obsessed with his eating behaviour. Sometimes toddlers pick up on this vibe and the pressure to eat makes them get stubborn. It is also important to look at what he is eating or drinking in the morning. If he's been drinking a huge beaker of juice and a plate of biscuits in the morning, he may just not feel hungry at lunchtime. Your toddler may need a small snack and water mid-morning, but he doesn't need to be able to graze constantly.

Toddlers are also very easily distracted and usually want to keep playing. Keep lunchtime short, with minimal distraction, and, if possible, try to eat lunch with him to keep him company. Try not to worry; as long as he is growing and doesn't seem to be in pain after eating he should be okay.

Q: My toddler only eats the same foods, day in, day out. What can I do to improve his diet?

A: It can be really stressful if your toddler will only eat e.g., yoghurt and rejects everything else. Try not to communicate your anxiety about this, and continue to offer other food along with his preferred food. Praise him if he will lick or try the food and it will help to break down any 'food phobia' that he may have developed. Try to be very matter-of-fact and calm and try to get your family to eat with him. If he's able to see you all getting on with your meals he won't feel under such scrutiny and may want to be part of the gang eating the good stuff.

Q: Should my toddler still have milk?

A: The Department of Health recommends that your toddler should drink full-fat whole milk until he is two years old. After his second birthday you can introduce semi-skimmed milk if that is more convenient. Skimmed milk isn't suitable for children under five.

Q: Should toddlers have vitamin supplements?

A: It's hard to provide all the nutrients that your toddler needs from his diet alone and so some vitamin supplements are a good idea. Many children in the UK are deficient in vitamin D due to the latitude we live at and the lack of sunshine. Your toddler cannot manufacture enough vitamin D in his skin between October and May, so a vitamin D drop is really important to prevent acute and chronic health problems. There are lots of vitamin supplements suitable for toddlers (your pharmacist can direct you to them).

---

real parent story

Cathleen (Cormack, 7 years, John, 5 years and Maddy, 2 years)

'My children seem to have no overlap in their favourite foods which makes things a bit tricky. I have a fruit lover, a carb fanatic and a meat eater. I make balanced meals and snacks but they don't eat them in a balanced way, but overall they do okay.'

Quiz: Is your toddler a picky eater?

There are so many factors that affect whether your toddler is a 'picky' eater that it can help to think around your own attitudes to food, what you like to eat, what flavours your toddler has been exposed to, and how you cope with your toddler's behaviour around food. Toddlers as a group can be fairly maddening to cook for with a normal neophobia phase, strong impulses and preferences for archetypal foods (so a broken biscuit isn't a proper biscuit). This quiz isn't supposed to feel like a criticism but rather to help reassure you that it's very common for toddlers to be a bit picky about what they eat and to help you think about positive and negative attitudes to food in your home.

1. Was your toddler:
   a) Exclusively breastfed for six months.
   b) Mixed formula and breastmilk in the first six months.
   c) Exclusively formula fed.

2. When you give your toddler a new flavour to taste does he:
   a) Notice and enjoy the difference.
   b) Sometimes enjoy new flavours.
   c) Reject and spit out new flavours.

3. During the week does your toddler:
   a) Happily eat whatever you buy and cook, so his food intake changes frequently.
   b) Eat a few different things each day and week but has a fail-safe group of favourite foods that you tend to provide.
   c) Insist on the same foods for breakfast, lunch, dinner and snacks.

4. What is your toddler's emotion during mealtimes?
   a) Happy and relaxed and happy to go with the flow.
   b) Is mainly happy during mealtimes, but is reassured by routine and recognised meals. May get upset with new foods or new places to eat.
   c) Gets very anxious or angry if new foods are given or if food is prepared in a different way.

5. How does your toddler react to a broken biscuit?
   a) They all taste the same so hardly notices.

b) Much prefers a full biscuit but will eat a broken biscuit if that's all that's available.

c) Is inconsolable if a biscuit breaks and will not eat broken biscuits or parts of complete foods.

6. Does your toddler have any rituals around food?
   a) As long as meals are provided he's happy.
   b) He has a favourite cup and plate but is fine if they are not available.
   c) He has to have the right cup and plate or can get upset.

7. What do you like to eat?
   a) I eat everything and really enjoy trying new flavours and cuisines.
   b) I tend to eat the same kinds of food but will try some new things.
   c) I am very picky myself and don't like strong flavours or new cuisines.

8. How do you react to your toddler at mealtimes if he's unhappy?
   a) Lots of smiling, reassurance and side-tracking with chatting.
   b) I'll find out what the problem is and change something if I can.
   c) I feel like I'm walking on eggshells and feel anxious around his meals in case something isn't right for him.

9. What happens when you give your toddler something you don't like to eat?
   a) I can't think of any food that I don't like.
   b) I try to give him things I don't like but I think my face shows that I don't really like them myself.
   c) I'm pretty picky myself so I tend to give him things I like or if I do give him something I don't like I tell him and pull a disgusted face.

10. What are your rules around finishing meals?
   a) I never insist on meals being finished and try to respect my toddler's fullness and hunger cues; he won't starve.
   b) It's depressing scraping food into the bin so I try to make my toddler finish some meals.
   c) I decide when my toddler has finished and don't let him get down from the highchair or table until I'm satisfied with what has been eaten.

Mostly As: Your toddler is not picky about food. He may have been exposed to a wide range of flavours in breastmilk and meals which have helped his palate to develop. He is probably quite relaxed and doesn't worry about broken biscuits or needing the right cup or plate.

Mostly Bs: Your toddler has fairly standard toddler attitudes to food and mealtimes. You are fairly relaxed around food and most of the time he isn't too picky but sometimes he can be very stubborn about rejecting food. Try to maintain your usual relaxed attitude and be patient around the occasional wobble.

Mostly Cs: Your toddler is a picky eater and may be anxious around mealtimes. It is really hard to relax in this situation, but it will really help your toddler not to develop anxious habits around food. Try to eat with your toddler and model a happy and adventurous attitude to food. Don't pull disgust faces when you offer foods you don't like and praise him (not in an over-the-top way) when he tries new foods.

TOP TIP

Put a new food on your toddler's plate every day for at least a week. Don't insist he eats it. By the end of the week he won't see the food as new and may be happy to try a taste.

chapter nineteen

sleep

'O Sleep, O gentle Sleep. Nature's soft nurse, how have I frightened thee...'

Henry IV, Shakespeare

I should begin this chapter by stating for the record that I woke up with my six-year-old in my bed this morning. This is by no means rare for our family and I do not think it is very rare for children of a variety of ages to seek out the 'big bed' for some or all of the night.

Some parents will proudly announce that their child sleeps from 7pm to 7am, always has and always will. What is harder to ascertain is if these mythical sleeping beings were born that way or made that way, or a mixture of the two.

I think our expectations of how our babies and toddlers should sleep are ludicrously high. Even toddlers that do sleep well will go through periods of illness, teething, developmental changes, moving to a big bed and holidays that disrupt their sleep.

In some ways it's much tougher for parents of toddlers that don't sleep through the night than for parents of babies. Toddlers are more mobile and more verbal than babies, and often suffer with night terrors and nightmares. There is also a lot of PPP (Parent Peer Pressure) about what is socially acceptable in terms of toddlers and sleep.

The science of sleep

By the age of two, most toddlers have slept for longer than they have been awake and will go on to spend two-fifths of their toddlerhood asleep. Sleep is particularly important for toddlers as it directly affects their development.

There seems to be evidence that early birds or night owls are born rather than made. In addition, anecdotally, generally being a 'good sleeper' seems to be inherited, with good sleepers saying that their babies are good sleepers and insomniacs fearing they have passed on the trait to their wakeful babies. It's hard to conclude anything from personal reports alone, however.

One difference among babies that is known is that small babies are more likely to need to wake for feeds when they are older. My three babies were all premature and small for dates, and I was encouraged to continue night feeds for longer than their larger peers. This inevitably led to night waking persisting, when bigger babies had one milk feed and slept through from a much earlier age.

There is also a variation in the temperaments of babies, with parents tending to report that their 'placid' babies are good sleepers whilst parents with more 'irritable' babies report that when they come into light sleep they wake up and call out.

The importance of sleep for learning

A study from Tel Aviv reported that children who had an extra hour of sleep, compared to their peers, performed better in memory tests, non-verbal reasoning tests, and general tests of IQ. In parallel, those children denied an hour of sleep performed worse. This study demonstrated a direct link with hours of sleep and some intellectual capacities.

Bearing in mind that we all know instinctively how important sleep is and know how dreadful we feel as adults when we are sleep-deprived, there is compelling evidence that modern life and sleep deprivation may have effects on children's learning and development over time.

For this reason I would not recommend being complacent and assuming that your toddler just needs less sleep than other toddlers. Just because a toddler is wakeful for longer periods and seeming to cope doesn't mean they are not sleep-deprived.

How much sleep does my toddler need?

The amount of sleep your toddler needs changes over time. The Department of Health recommends the following number of hours of sleep:

Around first birthday: 2½ hour of naps and 11 hours at night
Around second birthday: 1½ hours of naps and 11½ hours at night
Around third birthday: 0 to 45 minutes (a daytime nap will probably be dropped at some point this year). 11½ to 12 hours at night.
Around fourth birthday: 11.5 hours at night.

To avoid sleep deprivation, make sure that your toddler is getting the right amount of naps and sleep for her age. Try and keep your toddler's bedtime routine at the same time every night and the same for waking time. As tempting as it might be, don't try and catch up on sleep with weekend lie-ins. You will get more sleep overall if you can maintain the same pattern of sleep each day.

Melatonin

We live on a planet that has night-time and daytime. Life on earth has different life strategies; some organisms are active at night (nocturnal) and some organisms are active in daylight (diurnal).

Melatonin is a hormone found in animals, plants, fungi and bacteria in anticipation of the daily onset of darkness. It is the sleep hormone and we need darkness to encourage its production to ultimately encourage sleep.

Melatonin is synthesised from the amino acid tryptophan. Tryptophan is found in porridge, turkey, milk and bananas and these foods are recommended to promote sleep (see page 229). It is secreted by the pineal gland (or third eye) in a direct response to light patterns perceived by the eyes.

Cortisol

If melatonin is associated with the onset of darkness, then cortisol is associated with wakefulness and light. Cortisol is a hormone secreted by the adrenal glands (just above the kidneys) and has a hugely important role in sleep and body repair. When our circulating levels of cortisol are low our bodies can relax, recuperate and repair.

The cortisol awakening response happens after we wake up and it sees a 50 per cent increase in circulating cortisol. Cortisol and melatonin together help to regulate wakefulness (higher cortisol) and sleepiness (higher melatonin) and they practically mirror each other in their release into the bloodstream every 24 hours.

Types of sleep

When we sleep, our bodies are still and our brains go through cycles of sleep. By toddlerhood each full sleep cycle is around 90 minutes long and alternates between Rapid Eye Movement Sleep (REM, or dream sleep) – named literally by whether one can see the sleeper's eyes dancing around under their closed eyelids – and Non-rapid Eye Movement Sleep (NREM, or restorative sleep).

During REM sleep our bodies become still yet our sleeping brains are very active and we dream. During NREM restorative sleep our bodies are repaired and grow (as hormones are released) and our brain (to use a computer analogy) is shut down.

After each full sleep cycle your toddler will come into light sleep where she unconsciously 'checks' that the environment is safe and the same as when she went to sleep.

Hours of sleep

Toddlers do a lot of sleeping, and by 18 months this has been consolidated to one night-time sleep session, with much shorter daytime naps. In the second year of life, toddlers require between 11 and 14 hours of sleep every 24 hours (so more sleep than wakefulness).

By 18 months of age toddlers may only need one 1–3-hour nap a day. It's important to their night-time sleep that this nap isn't too early in the day. If your toddler wants a nap before 10am it usually means you have an early riser and the final dawn sleep has been broken away from the night-time sleep. Earlier bedtimes and delaying this early nap can help to prevent your toddler from waking too early. It may take a couple of weeks to achieve this.

It's also important that your toddler's nap is over by 3pm so as not to impact or delay their bedtime. This might mean trying to avoid sleepy car journeys or pram trips in the late afternoon.

Modern technology and sleep

Modern life is very good at sabotaging sleep. In the prehistoric past it was straightforward for our ancestors: when the sun went down it was dark and cool, they produced melatonin and slept, and woke with the dawn.

Compare this with the modern situation. The sun goes down and we put on electric lights, televisions and devices. This means a toddler in the 21st century has the following sleep enemies to deal with:

- electric lights that suppress her melatonin production
- tablets, televisions and smartphones; these emit a blue light which inhibits melatonin production
- a hot, centrally heated room stops her body from experiencing the slight temperature drop that promotes melatonin production

- outside street lighting and general light pollution mean for all but the most rural-living toddlers she never experiences real darkness
- adults watch television downstairs and the phone may ring in the evening. If your toddler is in light sleep mode when this happens, she may well be woken up, especially in an open-plan home. When she wakes she finds her parents awake, up and about, and bathed in light. Then we ask her to go back to her dark room alone. No wonder they often protest
- she is alone at night.

I am not advocating that we all return to the wilds, live in caves, and go to sleep at sundown with our toddlers. Instead, by appreciating how modern life disrupts your toddler's sleep by understanding the triggers, you can make their evenings, nights and sleeping areas more conducive to sleep for everyone.

The importance of a bedtime routine

My number one top tip for improving your toddler's sleep is to introduce a bedtime routine that starts in the early evening. We are creatures of habit, and it is really helpful to have a bedtime routine to help trigger sleepiness. By routine I mean a series of events that always happen in the same order, in the same place. Each step leads on to the next step and facilitates sleepiness.

TOP TIPS TO PROMOTE YOUR TODDLER'S SLEEP

Your toddler's sleep is important, and here are some ideas you can use to help her have calm bedtimes and restful sleep, based on the science of sleep:
- it is vitally important that your toddler does not play on tablets or smartphones two hours before bedtime

- ideally, the bedtime and bathtime routine should take no longer than 30 minutes from start to finish, so your toddler can best benefit from the melatonin released by her drop in body temperature after a bath. So: quick bath, get into bedclothes, bedtime milk, teeth clean, and into bed for a relaxing story
- if your toddler has something to eat in the evening before bathtime I would suggest tryptophan-rich foods like porridge and bananas
- give her a short, warm bath (not hours of playing in the evening). The drop in temperature she will feel climbing out of the bath will promote melatonin production and sleepiness so you need to move on with her bedtime routine promptly after bathtime
- make sure her bedroom is gently lit (a red-based light is better than a blue-based); don't take her back downstairs to the bright lights, television and food
- read her a relaxing bedtime story; try to avoid acting out the whole of *We're going on a bear hunt* at this time – save those exhilarating stories with lots of funny voices and sound effects for the daytime. I recommend a bedroom book collection and a living room book collection to make the selection easier
- give your toddler a comforter that she associates with bedtime and acts as a trigger for sleep; this can be especially helpful to encourage your toddler to sleep in her own bed, or when staying in a new place
- if you like, lie next to your toddler, cuddle her and breathe slowly. Your toddler will subconsciously breathe-match you which will help her to relax and be able to fall asleep soon.

Beds, cots and sleeping bags

Toddler beds can be a new and exciting stage for your toddler and many toddlers take to them with great gusto (although as I did a lot of lying next to my toddlers I found them a bit uncomfortable).

However, if your toddler drops off easily and sleeps through the night they can be the best of both worlds; a safe transition from a cot in that they are close to the ground and have a guard around the head area to help prevent your toddler from falling out of bed.

In my family, as we were tight on space we ended up with bunk beds. The problem with bunk beds is that they make cuddles and bedtime stories difficult for the child in the bottom bunk, and impossible for the child in the top bunk. Obviously it's possible to read a bedtime story elsewhere, but I still feel it is a huge downside. I think, in part, this is why I welcome my children into our big bed as it's too hard to cuddle them in their narrow bunk beds.

Travel cots

These can be useful when away from home; look out for the design that allows you to place your baby inside from the side. I have to say that I hate those travel cots with high sides, partly because my babies and toddlers would never go down in them, so I ended up having to lift them in and lift them out which was difficult.

Sleeping bags

Child-sized sleeping bags are great if your toddler kicks off her covers and gets cold in the night, but not great if your toddler gets twisted up in them and wakes up as a consequence. Lots of parents swear by them as they are cosy and stop your toddler getting undressed at night. If your toddler is used to them as a baby you can be pretty sure they will suit them as a toddler. When your toddler is more settled at night you may make the move to a light duvet but be prepared to pop it back on the bed now and then!

Blackout blinds and night lights

If you live in the city or have a street light outside your home, blackout blinds can make a huge difference to the ambient light in your toddler's bedroom or sleeping area. You may also need to buy travel blackout blinds with window suckers when you travel – many a parent has been stumped when their toddler can't sleep on a holiday or a visit to grandparents, as the exact same dark room can't be replicated.

If your toddler begins to be scared of monsters or the dark, a night light (either on the landing near the loo, or in her room) can help reassure her. Try and get one with a warm red-based light to minimise disruption of melatonin production (light at the blue end of the spectrum suppresses melatonin production much more).

Co-sleeping

Nurseries, cots and children's bedrooms only appeared in human history relatively recently. Before that, protecting our young was a 24/7 job and we slept together to keep warm and to keep safe. Indeed, the Department of Health recommends that babies sleep in their parents' room for the first six months, as breathing next to parents regulates the child's breathing.

If you look at the anthropology of sleep over the ages, babies and toddlers have always been close to parents at night and slept close by. For this reason I have always been happy to snooze with my toddlers at their bedtime. If they wake up later in the evening I will lie with them again. They often then slept in their own bed and then came and slept in my bed, and I made my peace with that. Co-sleeping, either proudly announced or secretly endured, is a very common part of both the ancient and modern anthropology of sleep. When you accept that co-sleeping will be part of your life it makes your toddler's sleeping much easier and less fraught.

However, that is not to say that it is right for everyone by any means. You, your partner or your toddler may not want to co-sleep at all, and your toddler may well sleep very happily in her own toddler bed in her own room. In my family, my son has always fallen asleep before my daughters and then slept very deeply. He sleeps worse if he's sharing a bed with someone. He didn't have any overt differences in how we responded to him at night – he's just a good, happy solo sleeper.

Co-sleeping can include sharing the same bed or having a sleeping area attached to the main bed. There are some well-established safety recommendations which focus on reducing the risk of SIDS (Sudden Infant Death Syndrome) in babies which are still good practice if you do decide to co-sleep with your toddler:

- neither you or your partner should have smoked, drunk alcohol, or taken any prescription or recreational drugs prior to bed-sharing
- you need a firm mattress. Waterbeds and memory foam mattresses are not recommended for bed-sharing or suitable for babies and toddlers
- only borrow sleeping equipment which still has the manufacturer's instructions
- big pillows, duvets and blankets are not recommended as your toddler can slither down under them – you and your toddler will need light bedclothes
- your toddler should sleep next to one of you and not between two adults (there is evidence that mums are able to rouse and sense their child coming into light sleep and are less likely to roll on their child than other adults)
- your toddler should not sleep next to other siblings
- do not co-sleep if you are deeply sleep-deprived as this may diminish your ability to respond to your toddler in the night, and increase the danger of you not waking if you roll onto your toddler

- if you or your partner are overweight, a bed space next to, or near your bed might be a safer solution
- a low bed, mattress or futon is best to prevent the danger of your toddler rolling out of bed.

Benefits of co-sleeping

In my experience the main benefits of co-sleeping include:

- more hugs and cuddles for your toddler (and you!)
- when your toddler wakes up, you are there and can quickly soothe her back to sleep without any drama
- it's easier to nurse a poorly toddler when you co-sleep with them, and I would recommend it even if generally you and your toddler don't co-sleep
- toddlers often drop off and sleep much more soundly when they are able to co-sleep with you.

Sickness and co-sleeping

All children tend to save their peak illness for the dead of night – generally around 3am. This is when you are most tired and there are no doctors around. This is when being a parent and nursing them literally becomes a 24/7 job. It's exhausting, and co-sleeping not only makes it easier but I can confidently state that on two occasions I have got a vital early warning that my children were dangerously ill because they were in my bed.

On the first occasion I called my mum and told her that my eldest was very mottled and had pale lips at bedtime. Quite unusually, my mum said 'stay with her tonight'. She might have saved my daughter's life, as in the middle of the night I became aware that something was wrong ... maybe it was my subconscious feeling a change in her breathing rate or her temperature. Whatever it was, I sat bolt upright. She was very cold and was completely unresponsive to me for two hours. She was taken by ambulance to hospital and transferred to a paediatric ward.

Her temperature started to spike at over 42 degrees, she was put on intravenous antibiotics and thankfully began to recognise me again (she had a severe adenovirus and went on to develop autoimmune neutropenia). I dread to think what would have happened if she had been sleeping in another room away from me. I woke up and looked after her because I sensed something.

On the second occasion, my son had a big drop in temperature after a febrile seizure and again I woke up. He had a tiny, non-blanching rash on his body. We got him to hospital and he was treated for suspected meningitis within 20 minutes of my sensing something was wrong.

For this reason I would always recommend bringing your toddler into bed with you when he or she is poorly. However, the same rules apply as mentioned before and you should not co-sleep if you or your partner are a smoker, or if either of you have drunk alcohol or taken drugs.

Downsides of co-sleeping

There are downsides to co-sleeping – mainly for you as a parent. Toddlers have the ability to take up huge amounts of room. Parents can end up perched on the edge of their bed with their toddler lying in various area-maximising positions (starfish position, foot in Mum's face, and hand in Dad's ear etc.). However, sleep deprivation is not funny and if you, your partner or your toddler's sleep is being too disrupted by sharing a bed you may want to try your toddler sleeping in her own bed space, bed or room.

Many couples feel that co-sleeping impacts their sex life, though many pro co-sleeping parents recommend having sex outside the bedroom.

Unlike in many parts of the world, there is a stigma in the UK to co-sleeping with your children, that in some way it's a failure, it will ruin your toddler's sleep habits, or kill your marriage etc. Parents with young families are very vulnerable to this kind of censure. If I could speak to my sleep-deprived self when

I had toddlers I would say: 'ignore the critical voices, if you all get a good night's sleep co-sleeping, then do it, don't worry as all your children will go on to sleep through the night ... just like their peers.'

Meeting your toddler's needs at night

There is a lot of importance placed on meeting your child's needs at night. Some children may like to play with your hair as they drop off; one of mine liked to pinch at my throat, which worked for her but was painful and irritating for me. I think when it comes to these soothing behaviours you need to think about what you are, and are not, willing to enable. My youngest actually learned fairly quickly to fall asleep without the throat grabbing, though it required consistent removal of her hand. I wish I'd realised this earlier but I was tired and sleep-deprived.

Toddlers do not need nutrition at night, so based on that fact you may decide that feeding at night isn't needed. However, breastfeeding is more than just nutrition and many (especially young toddlers) may still breastfeed at night. If you are co-sleeping and feeding lying down, some toddlers may latch on to feed and drop off and no one is disturbed. Many parents do want to wean their toddler from breastfeeding and this might start with night feeds. This can be really tough for mum and toddler, so do it gradually, starting with one feed, and try to soothe your toddler back to sleep without a breastfeed. It can sometimes help if your partner soothes your toddler as she will not expect a breastfeed from him. Make sure that you minimise the chances that your toddler will wake at night to avoid the desire to feed at all: make sure she is comfortably dressed, her room should be a nice temperature (around 18 degrees), and don't let your toddler go to bed hungry.

Sleep training

Sleep training works on the premise that it's the child's behaviour or 'sleep associations' that need to be changed. In many methods the child's physiology or emotional needs are not considered, which is a major flaw in my mind.

'Controlled crying' sleep training involves leaving your toddler to cry for a period of time, then going in after a few minutes to be present and soothe without cuddling or feeding your toddler. The idea is to teach your toddler to go back to sleep without help from you. It is arguably 'effective' at stopping toddlers and babies crying in the night when they wake or come into light sleep. However, in my experience most 'sleep-trained' toddlers I knew needed lots of training over time. This wasn't a one-time training that worked forever. More worrying there is physiological evidence that babies who are left to cry by themselves without being soothed may be stressed even as they remain silent.

Cortisol (see page 228) is also referred to as a stress hormone, and its production can prevent sleep, and has implications for such sleep-training methods. A study that tested the salivary cortisol levels of babies who were being sleep-trained reported raised levels after the training, even in quiet babies that were no longer crying.

The reason that high levels of cortisol are not desirable is that the stress hormone curbs resting and restorative functions that are put on hold in a real fight-or-flight situation. Cortisol dampens the immune system and suppresses the digestive system and growth and repair. Prolonged cortisol bathing the developing brain in this way also may affect the parts of the brain that control mood, motivation and fear.

The perfect study into the effects of sleep-training methods has not been carried out – largely because it would be unethical. However, there is a growing body of scientific evidence that even when 'sleep-trained' babies and toddlers no longer cry when left alone at bedtime, this is not associated with low cortisol levels (i.e. these quiet babies are still stressed but are no longer communicating it to their parents as they have learned that their parents do not respond to their cries). These elevated cortisol levels (usually tested by a simple salivary cortisol test) indicate that the child is stressed.

This is particularly worrying as central to the connection between a parent and a child is that they are in emotional sync, and it is upsetting to think that a parent may feel relaxed and happy as their toddler remains quiet in bed but that their toddler's stress is now hidden from them as a direct result of sleep training.

My children are now all at school and if I could have my time again I would have trusted my instincts and not attempted my few, half-hearted and anguish-filled attempts at 'controlled crying'. I know several children who were sleep trained fairly successfully and appear to be happy and secure but the potential long-term effects of what could be argued is a traumatic event for a baby are not yet well understood. However, it's important not to dismiss them just because the studies haven't been done yet – I would prefer to err on the side of caution. There is just so much evidence that supportive and responsive parenting sits at the centre of a child's mental health to prevent or reverse chronic stress – so supportive and responsive parenting at night is likely to be just as valuable to a child's emotional development.

Furthermore, like in the case of smacking, it is the parent or attachment figure and their distance (or short-term abandonment) that is the source of the stress and the sadness which is particularly hard for a toddler to process (see the chapter on positive discipline for a greater discussion of this factor).

I would not recommend sleep-training methods that involve leaving your toddler to cry by themselves so that they learn to fall asleep without any help. However, I know that some parents are at breaking point. They may be dealing with depression, breakdown of the relationship, new babies and sleep deprivation. These are all terribly difficult problems that need to be borne in mind as well as your relationship with your toddler and their needs. If possible my recommendation would be for a good consistent bedtime routine with cuddles. Some toddlers will go off to sleep on their own and some will want to be soothed to sleep; if the latter you can either choose to co-sleep or just soothe them to sleep in their own bed space.

In hindsight I would have loved to have had a book that I could read with my husband that gave us 'permission' to co-sleep and helped explain why sleep training felt so bad. Armed with this knowledge I think we would have had more realistic expectations about our toddlers' sleeping behaviour and not have felt like failures when we soothed our toddlers at night.

Caveats

YOUR TODDLER'S SLEEP AND YOUR RELATIONSHIP

As a married mother of three children I in no way underestimate the negative impact that a toddler that wakes a lot or sleeps in your bed can have on your relationship. I know many of my friends, myself included, who in desperation tried controlled crying, had huge rows with their partner as everyone was sleep-deprived and at the end of their tether. Mums in particular can often feel like they have to choose between their toddler and their partner and end up trying sleep-training techniques that make every instinct in their bones scream 'no'. I, like many mums, have sat crying at the bottom of the stairs whilst my partner takes over 'teaching our toddler to sleep' and it was miserable. If you have a toddler who doesn't fall asleep quickly it is heart-wrenching to hear your toddler crying out for you.

With hindsight I wish I'd never tried it, it didn't work for us, my babies were deeply upset, I was deeply upset and my partner was deeply upset. So a 'lose, lose, lose' scenario for me. However, I remember how desperate I was for a solution and like many parents I bought lots of books with miracle titles. For this reason I would never condemn a desperate sleep-deprived parent. I think that experts, parents and grandparents should be more honest about their toddler's sleep and should have more realistic expectations about their toddler's sleep and the price that has to be paid if you choose to prioritise sleep over other aspects of your toddler's emotional development.

Your toddler's sleep and your other children

One of the challenges of having more than one child is that one child's needs around sleep can impact your other child's sleep. In an ideal world I, like the Jolie-Pitts, would have loved a big nine-foot-wide bed that could accommodate any and all of the family. However, the safety advice is that older children shouldn't sleep next to babies and toddlers (don't let your toddler sleep next to a baby as they may roll over and suffocate them).

In an ideal world you could try to really focus on consolidating your toddler's sleep well before a new baby comes along, because your baby will need feeding in the night and will need to be seen to first. I have found that co-sleeping can help as I have been able to lie down to feed my baby and have my toddler behind me – who will feel comforted by my proximity. Try to encourage your toddler to have a teddy or comforter at night to help soothe them when you can't give them your full attention.

Your toddler's sleep and your work

The desperation of a working parent to have a good night of sleep before getting up, getting out and getting to work is strong.

If you are going back to work again you will need to slowly work towards improving your toddler's sleep. Make sure your toddler's bedtime routine starts early so that you can have an early night too. Follow all the advice on making her bedroom or sleeping space comfortable, dark, cool and conducive to sleep. It might be tempting to keep your toddler up late if one or both of you haven't seen her today but this will have an impact on her sleep.

You may feel like all the other parents at work are sorted and their babies, toddlers and children all sleep for an unbroken 12-hour period – but don't bet on it. We are all generally coping with disrupted sleep and being honest with your friends and (close) colleagues can help to reduce the pressure.

Night terrors and nightmares

Night terrors and nightmares are different things. Whereas nightmares occur during rapid eye movement sleep (REM), night terrors occur during deep sleep and are not based around a dream. Night terrors happen usually in the first three hours of sleep and your toddler has no memory of a dream (because there wasn't one). After a nightmare, conversely, your toddler might stutter out a word about what was in the bad dream.

If she is experiencing a night terror, and calling out or thrashing around, try not to wake her up and interact with her; just see if she will go back to sleep. The Department of Health recommends waking a child when the night terror finishes, to soothe her and maybe taking her for a wee. This prevents your toddler from dropping back into deep sleep which can lead to another night terror episode straight away. Try not to worry; as long as she doesn't bump herself she won't be permanently damaged by a night terror.

If your toddler has nightmares and wakes up frightened, it is important to respond to her anxiety and fears and to soothe her. Nightmares are common because your toddler's brain and memory are developing, and with this burgeoning imagination comes a new fear of monsters and the unknown. It can really help a toddler to have a teddy bear or comforter as well as a night light. Respond to her distress with lots of cuddles and stroking her hair. You may have to repeat that you are there, the dream has gone and it was not real – until your toddler calms down or drops off back to sleep. The dream is unlikely to come back again as they will begin a new sleep cycle.

SLEEP DEPRIVATION AND OBESITY

In one study sleep researchers have reported that the less sleep a child is having the bigger his or her waist. Although correlation doesn't prove causation, there may be some hormonal reasons that connect eating behaviour with sleep. When

---

a toddler is severely sleep-deprived the usual production of melatonin at night-time is disrupted and leads to an imbalance in two hormones that regulate hunger and satiety: ghrelin and leptin (leptin is actually manufactured in fat tissue). Very simply, sleep-deprived toddlers have increased periods (especially when they should be sleeping) where their hormones are telling them they are hungry but they actually don't need to eat. This positive reinforcement leads to more fat deposition and an increase in hunger.

Snoring

When we fall asleep certain muscles in the airways relax and for some of us that means snoring. Snoring in toddlers is quite common, around one-fifth. Snoring can be caused by allergies, upper respiratory tract infections and even obesity (if there are lots of fat deposits around the neck). In 3 per cent of toddlers, snoring might be an early sign of 'obstructive sleep apnoea'. This small minority of toddlers have an extra cause of snoring that may highlight an underlying medical problem. This is because, at their age, they may have large adenoids and tonsils which can not only contribute to snoring but you may even notice that they stop breathing for a few seconds – this cessation of breathing is called sleep apnoea. Signs of obstructive sleep apnoea include:

- loud snoring
- pauses in breathing
- choking and snorting during sleep
- mouth breathing
- unusual sleep positions with their head either much higher or lower than their body
- morning headaches (these should always be checked out)
- tired crankiness in the morning

- hard to tie to the apnoea, but disrupted sleep can link to attention and behaviour problems and even delayed learning and development.

Your doctor may refer your toddler to a sleep laboratory where they will monitor their circulating oxygen levels as well as general tests of heart rate, blood pressure and breathing rate. Medical intervention can include grommets and tonsil removal.

> My nephew had huge adenoids and tonsils and his sleep apnoea was very alarming. He also had endless viruses, colds and glue ear. This had an impact on his hearing and sleep. Medical intervention with grommets and later tonsil and adenoid removal helped enormously so my advice is always insist on getting suspected sleep apnoea, lack of speech and constant ear infections checked out.

Sleep regression

'Sleep regression' is a big buzz phrase in child sleep books, though I never really felt my children had a position of sleep perfection to regress from. However, it is true to say that a toddler's sleep can change over time, and she may have phases of great sleeping and phases of very disrupted sleep. Some of these disruptions will be seasonal, some will be medical, and some with be developmental in origin.

Your toddler is learning and developing at super speed, and these sleep 'regressions' tend to happen around times of progress in your toddler's development. These may include jumps in language acquisition or fear of the dark.

Dutch behavioural researchers Frans Plooij and Hetty Van Der Rit have a lovely concept of 'wonder weeks' to describe critical periods of development where intense strides and changes are made in the way your toddler conceptualises and perceives the world. As a parent you will see many of these leaps; sometimes it's a big physical development, such as the ability to run, sometimes it's an emotional change, such as fear of the dark. Whatever the developmental jump is, it means that your toddler's brain is changing, rewiring, pruning and growing. Your child's brain doubled in weight from birth to first birthday, and by the age of two years it is 75 per cent of adult size. It will almost catch up in size with you by the age of five years. All this brain development and learning can result in broken sleep.

This is all very well, but even though you may be thrilled that all these sleepless nights are proof positive of your beloved toddler's blooming brain, it can seem like it is completely at the expense of your own addled cerebellum!

---

real parent story

Lance (Tommy, 14 months)

'I sleep like a log and my wife sleeps like a log and luckily Tommy seems to have inherited the sleeping genes. He was a big baby and slept through earlier than our friends' babies. Apart from when he was teething or sick, he's always fallen asleep and slept well. He used to babble in his cot in the morning quite happily. I don't think we did anything right – just lucky!'

Quiz: Is your home 'sleep friendly'?

This quiz is designed to help you see if you are making your toddler's bedtime routine, bedroom and night-time conducive to sleep. It might remind you about how calm, or not, bedtime is in your home.

1. How much natural light does your toddler see during the day?
   a) I don't really monitor it. If we go out to the shops or a soft play centre she gets some fresh air and daylight.
   b) My toddler goes to the park most days but in winter we have quite a few cosy days inside.
   c) My toddler plays outside every day for 2–3 hours a day, come rain or shine. We always have a play outside before dinnertime.

2. What is the temperature in your toddler's bath and bedroom?
   a) My toddler has a very cool bath and her bedroom is quite warm.
   b) My toddler has a long, warm bath with lots of toys to play with, and her bedroom is probably a little on the warm side.
   c) My toddler has a short warm bath and her bedroom is about 18°C.

3. What are the noise and light levels like around your toddler's bedtime routine?
   a) She has a bath then comes back and sits on my knee in the brightly lit sitting room for a story. Her bedroom isn't very dark.
   b) She has a bath and has a story in her bedroom which isn't very dark but is quiet.
   c) My toddler has a bath in low lights, then she has a story where she sleeps with a low light. The curtains have blackout blinds or are lined with blackouts so it's very dark.

4. How quiet and calm is your toddler's bedtime?
   a) We have a full home and every room has lights on in the evening. She plays on the iPad and watches television after her bath. When I get a moment, I quickly take her up to bed.
   b) We try to keep it down in the evening but the noise from the TV does carry upstairs sometimes.
   c) I like a technology-free evening, so after my toddler has gone to bed we tend to read.

5. What does your toddler cuddle at bedtime?
   a) She doesn't use a comforter or a cuddle but doesn't seem to mind.
   b) I don't give my toddler a night-time cuddle but she has a teddy/comforter that she cuddles herself.
   c) I lie next to my toddler and we breathe slowly together while we have a cuddle, and she clutches her teddy/comforter in her arms.

6. Does your toddler have a bedtime story?
   a) I'm generally too tired to read a story at night so we tend to give it a miss.
   b) My toddler has a big pile of stories by her bed, with lots of buttons to press and songs to sing.
   c) My toddler has a nice selection of gentle bedroom stories that I choose from. They help her to wind down and tend to be rhythmic and calming.

Mostly As: There are lots of stimulating factors in your toddler's bedtime routine that make it hard to trigger sleepiness and sleep. Try to remove as much stimulation as possible and include lots of daylight play in the afternoons. Run a warm bath and make sure her room is around 18°C.

Mostly Bs: You have some nice, calming triggers to help your toddler get restful sleep, but some factors that will overstimulate your toddler and wake her up again.

Mostly Cs: Your toddler's daytime activity and bedtime routine are conducive to triggering calmness and sleep. All toddlers are different, so if your toddler doesn't like a teddy don't insist on adding it into the bedtime routine.

chapter twenty

tantrums and positive discipline

'Do not train a child to learn by force or harshness; but direct them to it by what amuses their minds, so that you may be better able to discover with accuracy the peculiar bent of the genius of each.'

Plato

Discipline should not be about your ego; it is about teaching your toddler and helping him to understand the boundaries of acceptable and unacceptable behaviour. This needs to be put into the context of love, safety, empathy and respect for other people.

I don't advocate the 'naughty step', 'timeouts' or smacking. I think it is possible to be much more ambitious about how we teach our toddlers to behave, in a way that recognises how they think and feel.

There is a lot said or written about that toddlers are 'manipulative' and need discipline, but toddlers do not have the brain skills to pull the wool over their parents' eyes or manipulate them. They just react honestly. When you have a toddler, you can feel very judged by other adults as you try to cope and manage his behaviour, but try not to fall into the trap of 'being seen to parent' by playing the part of a strict/sorted/ super parent (delete as appropriate). We've all felt the pressure in front of friends, in-laws and healthcare professionals to treat our toddlers completely differently from how we would choose to treat them.

I remember delivering an ultimatum to my eldest child when she was a toddler. She wouldn't say sorry at the park so I loudly and proudly announced, in front of the other parents and my friends who were there, that if she didn't say sorry we would be going home. She didn't back down and so after only just arriving at the park on a beautiful day I found myself having to follow through my threat. It was a 'lose, lose' situation; I didn't want to go home either. My toddler didn't learn a lesson, she lost her temper, and I had put social evaluation by peers ahead of my relationship with my child. There are other ways to handle these situations. It's about having the confidence to be true to yourself as a parent: 'Parent', don't be 'Seen to Parent'.

In order to understand the best way to set calm and sensible limits and boundaries on your toddler's behaviour, it first helps to understand how your toddler's mind develops.

Mirror neurons, 'discipline' and learning

In 1992, Professor Giacomo Rizzolatti, a neuroscientist and doctor at the University of Parma, made an accidental discovery in his research on neurobiology in monkeys. He discovered that brain neurons associated with movement 'fired' when the monkey watched a scientist reaching for a peanut. The monkey's brain lit up the same way whether its body did an action or it watched another individual do that action.

With Rizzolatti's observation, the concept of 'mirror neurons' as a mechanism by which one animal learns from another was born. Since that first observation, mirror neurons, in conjunction with facial expressions, have been hypothesised to be the mechanism by which human beings feel empathy. In short, we feel empathy because when we see anguish on a person's face, our brains fire as if we feel anguish ourselves. Empathy, as opposed to sympathy, means understanding what others are feeling because you have experienced it yourself or can put yourself in their shoes. Empathy is a better way to help teach toddlers to behave with consideration, than hoping he will remember an arbitrary set of rules set by an autocratic parent.

Dan Siegel, a researcher at UCLA's School of Medicine, has written several books and led the movement known as 'interpersonal neurobiology' that uses the concept of mirror neurons. Interpersonal neurobiology treats the brain as a social organ, in the same way that the heart is a physical organ. This is a fusion of neurology and the emotional system that develops in relationships. In an attempt to more simply conceptualise the brain as a social organ, the brain is described in the classic triune description: the brain stem (which controls basic life functions like breathing); the limbic system (which is the feeling part of the brain that controls basic survival behaviours like aggression and fear); and the cerebral cortex (which is the thinking, rational brain).

Siegel explains that when a toddler is acting out and having a tantrum we are essentially dealing with the limbic, emotional or reptilian portion of our toddler's brain. If your toddler's limbic brain responds with aggression, then the limbic system of your brain may instinctively respond back in a 'reptilian face off'. So no one is thinking straight!

Toddlers are not able to regulate their emotions very effectively. A toddler's neo-frontal cortex is literally not fully grown; this final part of brain development doesn't occur until well into adulthood. Your role as a parent is to help your toddler to regulate his emotions until his own impulsive (limbic) brain doesn't have so much control. Shouting at him may just turn aggression into fear – and what lesson does that teach?

Tantrums can be pretty common. If you anticipate a meltdown you need to quickly take steps to defuse the frustration before your toddler loses control. Distract him with something compelling – point and say, for example: 'Can you see the aeroplane going over the trees?' This can change huge negative energy into huge positive energy almost instantly. You have successfully regulated your toddler's emotions and he will begin to relax, and then later you can have a calmer, warmer discussion about behaviour, if needed. He will be more receptive to your discussion then.

If the distraction doesn't work and your toddler continues to tantrum, just be there with him using calming, non-verbal stroking and body language until he starts to calm down. He will be feeling out of control and maybe even be frightened of his own feelings. Having you there with him is a huge emotional support and calming influence. Try to stay calm yourself which I realise is not always easy at the time, but it will help.

Our brains are well integrated (via nerves) with our body, and there are many feedback loops where the body impacts the brain. For example, when we feel anxious we get butterflies in our tummy which is, in turn, picked up by our brain and makes us feel more anxious!

Siegel encourages us all to look into our bodies and to teach our children to do the same. In the same way a meditating person does, we can, and should, train ourselves to use our 'mindsight' to assess and make sense of how we feel. This essential emotional tool should be central to teaching your child to be a true master of his own mind and body – what I think of as real, positive discipline. In order to help promote your toddler's 'mindsight' you can make sure that you have several times in the day where together you reflect on how you are both feeling and what has happened in the day. You need to schedule it into your daily routine; maybe after lunch or on the way to the park. Mindsight is hard brain work, so make sure that you don't relegate these important sessions to the times when your toddler is tired, hungry or fractious.

Smacking

It is emotionally confusing for a child when their attachment figure (usually the parents) is also a person who inflicts physical pain. This is because the limbic system senses danger and seeks safety in the arms of the attachment figure – but the attachment figure is the source of the danger in that moment. Put simply, it's hard for a child to absorb a meaningful lesson in the midst of this confusion, and it keeps the limbic system in charge without developing the 'muscle' of the newly growing and developing neo-cortex (the rational thinking part of the brain). A child simply can't understand the finer points of what you are 'trying' to teach when his brain is in fight or flight mode.

There is a lot of research evidence that smacking is not an effective form of discipline, and children who are smacked are statistically more likely to suffer from depression, commit suicide and end up in prison when they become adults. Again this is correlation rather than causation, and there is some evidence that smacking is often more prevalent in more chaotic families and chaotic communities.

Parents will often say that the only time they smacked their child was when they ran into the road. In this situation, what can we do instead? This is a life-or-death situation, and in that moment you need to respond quickly and remove the toddler from danger. However, as you both recover in the moment after the near miss you can regulate both of your shattered nerves. Explain how dangerous what he did was in a firm tone, and tell him how frightening that was for you. If you hit him, you shut down the conversation and lose the opportunity to teach him about road safety.

'Time out' and the 'naughty step'

Time out (where a child is taken to a quiet place to think about their bad behaviour alone) doesn't really give toddlers the opportunity to reflect, because at this age your toddler needs you there to help make sense of what he did and what he feels. Instead, he is more likely to feel frightened and try to shut down his feelings as he sits there alone.

In anger or fright, a toddler's limbic system is active, and he will often resist a time out. This often plays out, with the parent physically forcing the child multiple times to stay on the step. When the toddler does give up, and sink onto the step, he will not be in a reflective state.

Siegel has suggested an alternative to time out called 'time in' based on mindfulness. There is a groundswell of support amongst early years specialists and educators about the potential benefits of teaching mindfulness to children from a young age. Mindfulness training such as simple breathing and meditation time can have a hugely beneficial impact.

TOP TIP

If you would like to learn more about mindfulness, try a toddler and parent yoga class. There is often quiet meditation time at the end, and it's quite amazing to see a room full of little toddlers lying calm and quite, aware of their body and breath and tuning out the rest of the world.

Time in allows parents to help toddlers to regulate their emotions and become aware of how they are feeling. Time in doesn't happen in response to 'naughtiness', rather, like exercise or meditation, it becomes a consistent habit, a way of life and a daily emotional MOT.

This regulation and reflection can then prevent meltdowns and loss of emotional control.

A simple way to do this is to get into the habit of sharing your emotional response to an event with your toddler. So if a big dog ran up to you both and barked loudly, you retell the story and describe how you felt, such as 'shocked', 'scared' and 'worried'. As your toddler gets better able to describe the events in his own life, you can affirm by saying, e.g., 'Yes you really jumped, you must have felt frightened.' You can have this emotional discussion around all the flashpoints in the day and slowly teach your toddler to recognise his feelings in response to people, trials and tribulations.

INFECTIOUS YAWN TEST

Yawning is thought to be infectious due to the development of mirror neurons. Mirror neurons may help your toddler to copy and learn from others, and ultimately help us to understand how another person feels. Infectious yawning begins around the age of two, when children become more self-aware and aware of others. How does your toddler respond when you do a big pantomime yawn? If he yawns too it is a sign that he is attending to you and matching your behaviour, which is a sign of progressing emotional development.

real parent story

Jack (Max, 2½ years)

'When Max has a tantrum or is behaving badly I try to breathe slowly and speak calmly. It helps me to keep my cool and I'm convinced it relaxes him and ends the tantrum quickly. I'm not a pushover, I'm quite strict but I need to wait until he's calm and able to listen to me but I don't give in to hasten the end of a tantrum.'

Quiz: What is your parenting style?

This questionnaire is based on Dianne Baumrind's 'dimensions of parenting style'. Dianne Baumrind was very influential on both my research and my own parenting. She developed her idea based on two dimensions of parenting style – warm and sensitive to cold, and setting boundaries to no boundaries.

This led Baumrind to highlight three main parenting styles:

1. Authoritarian – warm, sensitive with boundaries.
2. Autocratic – cold, with boundaries.
3. Permissive – warm, sensitive with no boundaries.

A fourth would be: Neglectful – cold with no boundaries or interest, which has been identified by other psychologists.

Studies in the West have found that the children of authoritarian parents develop both self-esteem and self-control. The children of the neglectful parents are the most chaotic. The permissive parents tend to have less self-disciplined and more insecure children (due to the lack of boundaries and guidance) and autocratic parents tend to have less independent children. These parenting styles are based on a Western attitude to personal freedom and independence. It has been argued that some more collective societies would rate a strict autocratic parenting style as more acceptable.

1. How do you and your toddler talk?
   a) I listen when I must but I tend to tell him instructions mostly.
   b) We love our talking time and I feel I do lots of listening but I also lead the conversations.
   c) My life revolves around my talks with my child and I feel his contributions are just as valid as any other person's.

2. Your toddler wants to show you his dance just as your favourite television programme begins. What do you do?
   a) I'll tell him that he will have to wait to show me his dance when I am free to watch him.
   b) Well, I want to encourage him, so I'll watch the programme later.
   c) It means so much to him I turn off the television and watch him do his dance countless times and clap with enthusiasm.

3. Your toddler wants to do an activity that you aren't interested in, e.g. football.
   a) I decide what activities that my toddler attends so we won't go to this one.
   b) I'll let him do it at home but not join an official class until he's shown a real interest.
   c) I will make sure I sign him up if he wants to.

4. Your toddler wants to watch a grown-up programme.
   a) No. I don't want my child exposed to something that is too old for him
   b) No. I will explain that this programme is too scary and help him choose another activity that he likes.
   c) I'll let him watch to avoid a tantrum. I like the programme anyway.

5. Your toddler keeps opening a drawer that contains lots of potentially unsafe items, e.g. pins, scissors etc.
   a) No way, it's dangerous. He needs to learn that no means no!
   b) It makes him happy to explore, so I will remove the dangerous things from the drawer and let him explore.
   c) I'll let him explore if that's what he wants to do, I don't want a scene.

6. How much freedom do you allow your toddler at the park?
   a) I run things at the park, when he gives a turn to another child, what he plays on, how long we stay etc. He needs clear boundaries to keep him safe and sociable.
   b) I let him have a free rein, but will stop dangerous play or if he hurts another toddler.
   c) I let my toddler do what he wants at the park.

7. When judging what's best for your toddler, does your toddler have a say?
   a) No. He is too little and impulsive to make decisions yet.
   b) I give him choices that I decide from.
   c) I let him make his own decisions and his own mistakes as much as possible.

Mostly As: A for autocratic. You tend to prefer strict rules where you have control over your toddler's behaviour and activities.

Mostly Bs: B for authoritative. You are warm and sensitive to your toddler's needs, but see your role to regulate your toddler's behaviour and to set boundaries.

Mostly Cs: C for permissive. You love your toddler and find it difficult to say no to him.

TOP TIP

If you make 'time in' a part of your ongoing conversation with your toddler, you will feel the benefits with your own sharing, reflecting and emotional regulation too. Let's face it, being the parent of a toddler can lead to intense feelings of frustration, anger and sadness. I really think talking things through helps you both to connect, bond and keep each other on a more even keel.

part four

daily life with your toddler

In this part of the book you will learn about toddlers' relationships with the important people in her life, how she interacts with today's technology, and how best to keep her healthy and well.

toddler relationships

'When brothers agree, no fortress is so strong as their common life.'

Antisthenes

When your baby becomes a toddler she starts to form new relationships with people other than her parents. Forming relationships is both a vital skill in the life of a toddler and also helps to boost and support your toddler's emotional, cognitive and language development.

A new baby

The age gap between siblings is often around 18 to 24 months. This means that there are a lot of toddlers with newborn brothers or sisters. In some ways this is a tough time for a child to accept and love a new baby because they are still so young themselves. However, the good news is that there are lots of things you can do to lay the groundwork for a good transition from toddler to toddler plus one!

Your toddler will have lots of mixed emotions about the arrival of a new baby, from excitement and pride, to fear and anger. If your toddler was your first child she is used to being an only child and the centre of attention.

If she's not the oldest she will have got used to her role of being the baby of your family, but now she's about to be usurped by a new model (judging by the attention the arrival of her new sibling elicits from the adults in her life). She's been your baby her entire life and has never known anything else.

The change for her when a new baby arrives will be nothing short of monumental – someone once described it as like not only finding out that your partner is having an affair but that his mistress is moving in for life. I don't say this to panic you, but to prepare you for when your toddler displays a less than loving reaction to her new sibling.

Each toddler will react differently. This will depend on her temperament, the family dynamics, and the age gap between her and the new baby. Even if your toddler doesn't behave in a particularly negative way, she might feel a whole raft of negative emotions that she will struggle to articulate including:

- jealousy and resentment towards the baby
- confusion, with a mixture of both excitement and sadness about the new arrival
- anger and disappointment towards her parents.

Common behaviour in toddlers with a new sibling

Although your toddler will have a very strong inner emotional world she cannot yet articulate and express how she's feeling, so don't be surprised if she displays some behaviour that hints at her inner 'turmoil'. This classic behaviour includes:

- being baby-like in terms of both language and behaviour such as trying to breastfeed, crawling and pretend 'babyish' crying
- more tantrums
- physical aggression towards you and sometimes towards the baby. You need to supervise your toddler when she is with your baby at all times … she won't yet understand the implications of hurting the baby
- disruptive or attention-seeking behaviours
- she might 'internalise' her feelings and display more sadness and anxiety
- regression in sleeping behaviour and using the potty.

The good news is that with your help, and the help of everyone around you, these natural feelings will pass rather than become an ongoing problem.

Preparing your toddler for the baby's arrival

There is a lot to think about and lots you can do before your new baby arrives, so try to line up all your ducks:

- explain to your toddler while you are pregnant that she will have a new baby sister or brother in a time frame she understand, such as just after her birthday
- it's best not to insist that she will love the new baby, or announce that baby boys are just as fun as baby girls. This can lead to a confrontational style of discussion about the baby, and your toddler may become very stubborn and contrary in response
- explain that with a new baby comes disruption. One of the best ways to do this is by reading a book that illustrates (hopefully with charm and comedy) what it means to have a new baby around. *Topsy and Tim: The New Baby*, does a good job
- prepare your toddler for the logistical changes that will occur around the birth. For example, who will come and look after her while you are at the hospital, explaining you will be back soon
- read stories about being a big brother or sister – anything that shows how rewarding and enriching it can be
- if you're moving your toddler into a separate room so the baby can sleep in your room, do this well in advance so your toddler doesn't associate the new baby with being 'ejected' from their parents' room. If possible, try to make this a bit of a rite of passage with new bedding and bedroom furniture, or 'redecorating' with her own pictures
- don't start potty training around the arrival of the new baby. If you can, get it done first, but only if your toddler is ready (see page 195)

- get your toddler involved by taking her along to scans, choosing a name (maybe a second name!) and baby clothes
- when the baby is born, praise your toddler in all her attempts to help and be excited
- get your toddler a baby doll as a present from her baby brother or sister. This will put your baby in a good light, and your toddler can also buddy up with you so that you and your toddler can both carry your babies in a sling, bathe your babies, or breastfeed together
- along with the arrival of the new baby, give your toddler something she's been wanting for a while, something fun just for her, that feels quite 'grown-up' such as a tea set or scooter
- instil some early big brother or big sister responsibility by buying a present with your toddler for the new baby. Your toddler could bring it into hospital when she visits
- have some new toys and books (second-hand is fine) to give your toddler lots of new stimulation for those inevitable times when you have to focus on your new baby.

WHAT IF YOU HAVE TO STAY IN HOSPITAL?

New mums with a toddler at home can feel really torn and upset if they remain in hospital for longer than a day or so. If your baby is in NICU or SCUBU, have your toddler visit you frequently in hospital and, if appropriate, meet the baby. Use the visit to allow the person who brought your toddler along to cuddle the new baby giving you precious time to spend with your toddler.

Bringing home the new baby

Your toddler will probably be more excited to see you than the new baby, when you return from the hospital. She may have never spent a night without you before, and will need a big reunion and lots of reassurance. Try to have Grandma or someone else bring the baby inside so you can get down to your toddler's level and reunite. This may take several minutes, and when you judge the time to be right, you can introduce your baby to your toddler, e.g. this is your big sister and then 'show' the baby to your toddler, so she is the focus of the interaction (your baby won't care either way).

As your toddler gets used to the new baby, remember she is still young and egocentric, so put your baby in the context of your toddler. You might like to exclaim that they both have the same nose, for example. Explore the baby together in a loving and gentle way, e.g. ask your toddler to count how many tocs her new baby brother or sister has. In general, try and relate as much as you can to them.

Support from extended family

In a survey I undertook in my work with The Essential Parent Company, 90 per cent of parents lived over ten miles away from their extended family.

All new parents need lots of support from family and friends. This is even more the case if you have a toddler too, so try to have family and friends help. Your toddler will be thrilled if she can go out on a trip with a favourite relative, but you can also ask for your relative to mind the baby so you can spend some special time with your toddler.

In the Palaeolithic era, mothers would have had many more helpers in the form of older children, sisters and mothers or mothers-in-law. Try to bear this in mind and accept as much support from friends and family as works for you.

Visitors to the new baby

Remind visiting family and friends that it will help your toddler if they don't go all gooey-eyed over the baby and ignore your toddler in the clamour.

Ask close friends and family to bring a little gift for your toddler, especially if they are planning to come armed with presents for the baby.

real parent story

Katie (Fay, 20 months]

'One thing that I found really helpful was to totally shift the focus to Fay and make sure that everyone around did the same. So Ivan was always introduced as Fay's new baby brother and when people visited they would ask Fay to show them her new baby brother.'

Coping with a toddler and a baby

It is very common that your first child will graduate to toddlerhood around the time you have a new baby. It's exhausting even to think about meeting the needs of these two uniquely needy phases of life. I salute all parents looking after a babe in arms and a toddler round the ankles – even if it is common today. Very close age gaps would probably have been much rarer in our Palaeolithic past because longer exclusive breastfeeding (until two to four years) would have exerted a natural contraceptive effect that would have reduced conception during this period.

I think toddlers really benefit from having a baby sibling around. Life slows down with a baby, and toddlers are much less scheduled. Whilst both you and your toddler will at times be frustrated by the added needs of your new baby, parents are very good at looking after both children, such as learning to breastfeed in a rugby hold so that you can share a book with your toddler, or timing a trip to the park that allows baby to sleep while the toddler has fun.

What you lose in sleep and energy you can make up for in losing that mono-maniacal focus on one child. This tends to materialise as a more laissez-faire attitude to your children. For example, I think 'baby-led weaning' could be renamed 'I have a baby too' weaning. Gone are the perfect lump-free purées introducing different vegetables every 72 hours, and in come mountains of crushed potatoes and greens partly as you don't have the time to prepare anything else and partly to give you time whilst your toddler slowly and messily self-feeds.

I know that it is really tough when you need to focus on your toddler's needs or she needs help with potty learning and you feel like you need two of you. I recommend an 'order of events' routine around pressure points in the day, and also teamwork with your partner. Work out when you can feed baby and read to your toddler and stick to the times each day if you can; it just makes everything easier for you, and easier to process and learn for your toddler.

Toddlers do not need hundreds of scheduled events like swimming and ballet class to thrive. A slow walk with your baby sleeping in a sling while you chat about what you see will be probably more enriching and compelling.

real parent story

Sally (Harry, 22 months and Archie, 10 weeks)

'I was so worried about how Harry would feel when the new baby came but when Archie was born I hate to admit it but my mind was just full of Archie. Harry seemed big and old and for about 72 hours I just transferred all my focus onto this new baby. I was glad I was in hospital recovering from a C-section as it meant I could just be with Archie and I only saw Harry once a day. Then I came home and slowly got used to loving both my boys.'

Twin toddlers

Although this book is called *The Calm and Happy Toddler*, parents of twins have a whole different dimension to contend with if they have two toddlers simultaneously. Looking after two toddlers isn't simply having double the calls on your time, energy and patience. It's more than that.

Toddlers require a lot of attention and this produces a logistical problem. If you have two mobile toddlers, they can run in opposite directions so it's not possible to chase after them both at the same time.

One of my friends who has twins has a very relaxed and warm approach to parenting. However, she said that in order to survive with twin toddlers she had to instil stricter routines to prevent it becoming overwhelming. If you have twins I recommend you contact TAMBA (Twin and Multiple Birth Association) and accept support to help you with your twins or multiples during the toddler years. In time your children will be great playmates, but at the moment toddler twins are more than double the work of a singleton.

Grandparents and toddlers

'It takes a whole village to raise a child.'

African Proverb

Grandparents have such an important role in their grandchildren's lives that many evolutionary biologists (including my husband) have hypothesised that menopause (which is only found in humans and some whale species) evolved to produce Grandmas. Grandparents have stopped reproducing themselves and so in evolutionary terms are available to help out with their grandchildren. Sadly, many families don't live close together, but it's hugely important for you, your toddler and your parents to spend time together.

It would be naïve to claim that having grandparents around isn't without its difficulties for you as a parent.

Try to remember that what may feel like criticism is often based on love of your toddler, and in general toddlers benefit from having a relationship with their grandparents.

Grandparents can bring all those lovely stories and songs from your childhood to your toddler. It can be such a lovely time for them to rediscover the joy of children.

Toddler friendships

Young toddlers have rather limited social skills, but over the next year or two they will begin to form early friendships.

Play dates are great practice for learning to interact with a peer in a small and controlled environment. Your toddler will get practice at taking turns and experiencing that other people have a different view of the world. If your toddler is shy (see page 15) it's much easier for her if her first play date is with one other toddler at your home. Try to arrange a play date with a toddler who will play gently with your toddler and shares the same toddler interests, if possible.

Don't worry if your toddler seems to ignore her little friend on the play date, and instead plays her own game. This is called 'parallel play' and is a normal toddler stage with peers, as she won't yet see play as a shared experience.

When two toddlers come together you get two egocentric beings who act impulsively and who have little language to be able to interact and express themselves. Parents at toddler playgroups can sometimes feel like a cross between personal bodyguard and etiquette teacher who has to chaperone their own imperial highness around. Luckily, most parents of toddlers realise you are all in the same boat, and are quite good at working as a team to help toddler interactions run smoothly.

Toddlers and pets

Pets offer so many great opportunities for toddlers to learn, have fun, and let off some steam. A trustworthy pet can be a wonderful companion to a toddler, whether it's a cat that loves to be stroked, or a dog that matches your toddler for boundless energy on a walk – the bond can be very strong. Toddlers can talk to pets, play with them, and even begin to empathise with this non-verbal creature.

However, some pets are more suited to toddlers than others because toddlers are not very dexterous, gentle or empathic yet. Small pets such as mice and hamsters could be injured by your toddler so a large, slower-moving pet such as a cat or dog might be more suitable.

Toddlers should never be left alone with a large pet as they are unlikely to realise when a pet is getting aggressive, hungry or tired. Sadly, dog bites are not uncommon, with a quarter of a million people bitten by dogs in the UK alone every year.

It is worth taking care when out and about too: whilst it is good to encourage a relaxed attitude to dogs, it's not a good idea to let your toddler run up to strange dogs as her exuberant petting may not always be appreciated. Toddlers are often drawn to small dogs, and some breeds, such as Jack Russells, can be quite grumpy with strangers and nip. I was once not quick enough off the mark on the common next to where I live when my son was a toddler. An excitable puppy bounded past me to my toddler son (who was walking a couple of metres behind me) and jumped up on his shoulders, knocked him over and started jumping excitedly on him and licking his face. My son didn't know there was no danger, he was pinned to the ground by a large, strange animal and was terrified. He went on to develop a phobia of dogs which was only cured by a very patient and gentle Labradoodle called Milligan that lived on our street.

You will need to keep your toddler away from pet faeces, whether in a litter tray or out in the garden or park. There are rare cases of children being blinded by toxocariasis which is caused by roundworm parasites (toxocara) found in cat, dog and fox faeces. It's important to keep your pets regularly wormed and make sure your toddler learns how to wash her hands in warm soapy water before meals and snacks, especially after playing with pets.

The bond between toddler and pet

I am always staggered by quite how much my children love our cats and love the dogs that live in our street. They adore them and display such kindness and warmth around them. They really do see them as part of the family and develop complex relationships with them, involving lots of conversations and petting.

Cats, dogs and even chickens in the garden are very good for practising social skills, although it makes me laugh how toddlers love to order pets around. They enjoy the feeling of power; luckily dogs will accept their instructions and cats will just ignore them.

Health benefits of pets

Multiple pets have been shown to have a powerful preventative effect on a toddler developing allergies. A study supported by the American National Institute of Allergy and Infectious Diseases reported that toddlers exposed to two or more dogs or cats during the first 12 months of life were on average 66–77 per cent less likely to have any allergic antibodies to common allergens, compared with toddlers exposed to only one or no pets. This wasn't just a reduction in so-called pet allergies, but a reduction in a whole raft of allergies that plague modern toddlers. Subsequent studies have backed up this finding.

Furthermore, scientists in Finland reported that babies who spent up to six hours a day at home with a family dog had fewer ear infections, upper respiratory tract infections, and less need for antibiotics than babies who had no pets at home.

Hopefully these benefits reported in babies extend even if pets arrive on the scene later in a toddler's life too.

As I explain in the chapter on your toddler's developing immune system (see page 283) it seems that safe exposure to germs and allergens is an important part of training a healthy immune system.

Pets and autistic toddlers

A study from the Research Center for Human-Animal Interaction at the University of Missouri has reported that pets can really increase the social skills of children with a variety of development disabilities. It also found that pets are a great development aid for autistic toddlers.

Gretchen Carlisle, one of the authors of the study, explained that autistic children who lived with a pet or pets were significantly more likely to behave in social ways including:

- introducing themselves to new people
- asking for information
- answering questions.

She put the increase in these skills down to a global increase in their assertiveness. This increase in sociable behaviour was also observed when the children were in an environment with other people and animals.

Gretchen made the point that all children are individual and a dog would not necessarily be appropriate for all autistic children. See how your toddler reacts to a variety of animals before taking the plunge; asking friends with cats, dogs, guinea pigs, donkeys etc. to let you and your child visit and spend time with their pet.

TOP TIP

New baby?

Get together with other parents with new babies so that you can play tag team looking after the toddlers. Toddlers are social creatures and will usually happily take part or play with your friends' toddlers, so give them this chance to socialise, while you socialise with your friends and spend time with your baby.

toddlers and technology

'Computers tend to separate us from each other – Mum's on the laptop, Dad's on the iPad, teenagers are on Facebook, toddlers are on the DS, and so on.'

Tom Hodgkinson

One question I get asked more than any other nowadays is: 'Is it okay for my child to go on the iPad?' It's not surprising that parents worry. Devices such as iPads, iPhones and android tablets weren't invented when we were children and toddlers can seem like crack addicts when they get their hands on one. If left to their own devices, many toddlers would spend hours with a tablet gripped in their little hands. Tablets can provide wonderful learning experiences for children as well as evident entertainment. It is amazing to see how early toddlers can learn to play games on tablets with touch screens. Toddlers love to play on smartphones and tablets. With relatively little dexterity toddlers are able to swipe, press and interact with games long before they can speak fluently. The gadgets are very intuitive, and toddlers get constantly rewarded with very little frustration or need for help from an adult. However, before we embrace all the new technology with open arms, it's worth considering the impact that all this technology might have on your toddler's development and relationships.

Toddlers do not 'need' tablets or smartphones. Toddlers have developed and learned for thousands of years without them. The question many parents ask is does the positive outweigh the negative, or vice versa.

Professor Lydia Plowman is an education and development researcher at the University of Edinburgh who has looked at the pros and cons of a wide range of technological devices for children. She was invited by the Montessori movement to present her data on the effects of screen time for toddlers to help them to understand the impact of technology on child development.

Parents and educators tend to share the view that fresh air and learning through engagement with the physical environment is the natural and the best way that children develop. Seeing your toddler staring at a small blue screen and tapping it to feed an imaginary pet, can seem pointless and even harmful. This is especially worrying when our nation is seeing an epidemic in obesity in even very young children. Doctors recommend as much as three hours of physical activity a day for small children.

Worries about potential over-use of technology by toddlers is exacerbated by the guilt most busy parents feel when they allow their toddlers to use or play on tablets and smartphones to keep them quiet. Most parents of toddlers have handed over their smartphone whilst waiting in a busy waiting room to see the doctor, or so they can get chores done around the home.

I think this guilt does have a basis, and the way I've seen the best use of tablets is in collaboration between carer and toddler. Professor Plowman's research findings recommend that parents are present both physically and emotionally when their toddler is using technology. This shared experience is a really important part of using tablets and smartphones beneficially.

How does 'screen time' affect your toddler's development?

When toddlers are playing on screens, parents and experts have voiced concerns that this stunts their social and emotional development. I am aware that this makes me sound like a fuddy-duddy, but I've been shocked and depressed to see teenage couples on dinner dates where both have been absorbed in their phones, rather than talking to each other. If these teens are so addicted and shut off from the moment, what can we expect for our toddlers when they have probably had access to devices from a much earlier age?

Should we be worried about a dystopian future where the toddlers of today are plugged into some kind of matrix that means they don't see or connect with what, or who, is actually in front of them? Are there any benefits to a toddler's social development to be gained by using smart devices?

Professor Plowman's research leads her to be more optimistic: she found that devices can open up lots of communication potential in toddlers who cannot speak yet. This can help toddlers who may feel frustrated by being unable to communicate: 'Many young children don't yet communicate by reading and writing but are full of ideas that they want to express. This can be a really frustrating stage for them, but using technology in the right way can empower them to get their ideas across. This can be especially true for children with communication difficulties.'

I have a positive and a negative response to this conclusion. First, the positive one from a personal observation. My nephew suffered with moderate hearing loss as a baby and toddler, and was diagnosed with autism at the age of four. He has made cognitive leaps with the help of some of the fantastic developmental and learning apps available for tablets and smartphones. When he was completely non-verbal he was able to follow the pictographic instructions on many of these apps and was engaged whilst learning words, numbers and logical concepts.

I saw a talk by Ajit Narayanan who had developed a pictographic app that allowed non-verbal autistic children to communicate quite complicated language.

Secondly, the negative thought. Baby walkers were once hailed as a great way to help babies to learn to walk and help them get around and not feel frustrated. However, many developmental psychologists have argued that a baby or a toddler's brain development is most optimally encouraged by the natural trial and error that is part and parcel of learning to walk. If you effectively allow a non-walking baby to walk before their 'time' you will not be enhancing their development and their brain development will be out of sync with their overall physical development.

If we take this general point about synchrony across to the previous example of a non-verbal toddler able to use a device to communicate one cannot immediately conclude that this is better than the historical synchrony of emotional development, language acquisition and the hugely complicated physical development that allows toddlers to articulate their first sounds, words and sentences.

The most important way you can help your toddler to learn with devices is to share the game like you would share a book. If a game is non-verbal you have an important role in describing and explaining what your toddler is doing and achieving. When helping your toddler as she plays an app, think about all those things you do naturally with a story book. Your toddler gets lots of 'rewards' in the games whether it's collecting coins or completing a jigsaw. Her brain will literally 'give' her a dopamine reward which is why games are rewarding and addictive. However, your toddler will also be really pleased when you praise her concentration or tenacity at completing a task in a game:

- be interested in what the toddler is trying to achieve in the game: 'Wow, does the minion need to run all the way through this city to win?' 'Are the coins good to collect?'
- ask your toddler questions about the game: 'How many apples does Granny Smith need to eat?'
- suggest tactics or choice preferences in the game: 'Maybe this time you can make a green cupcake with a rainbow cherry on top!'
- help to regulate her emotions when she gets frustrated
- limit how much time your toddler spends playing a game by planning other activities before and after a session on a tablet, smartphone or other device
- keep it short – just five minutes a go. You need to keep an eye on this as the time can go by very quickly!

There are lots of great apps that are both elegant and compelling and teach children about:

- sorting and categorising
- cause and effect
- shapes and number
- words and sounds.

After you have played these games you can remind them of the skills covered, e.g. when asking your toddler to help you sort out the washing into piles of socks, knickers and T-shirts she will be using the same skills as she used in the sorting game, turning virtual fun into real-world skills.

Use of technology in daily life

I'm not a futurologist, but it seems that at some point children will benefit from being able to use the modern technology that they will encounter at school and in life. Unless you are opting for an Amish-style avoidance of electrical devices, you will need to decide when your children will be able to learn and master the devices in a safe and encouraging environment.

My youngest daughter loves to get involved with my online shopping. She loves to scroll through the list of our favourite foods and go to check the cupboards to see if we've run out of cornflakes or loo roll and need to get another one. It's always been a real treasure hunt task and we now use simple maths too, for example: 'Daddy eats tangerines all the time, but we only have three left so do you think we will need more for the next seven days?'

She also loves checking the weather at home and at her grandparent's home. Everyday apps can be just as fun and engaging as those specifically designed for children.

THE CALM AND HAPPY TODDLER

> ## 'GAME' APPS VERSUS 'EDUCATIONAL' APPS
>
> Don't assume that an educational app will be better than a game app (or indeed better than a more old-fashioned sticker workbook which has the added fine motor control skills of taking off the sticker and adding it to the right box). That said, there are a few absolutely fantastic word and number apps around.

> ## CHOOSING THE BEST APPS
>
> You need to check the content of any app before you download it. There are some really appalling apps (usually free) out there including those that have a questionable ethos such as where you reshape obese dolls (like a plastic surgeon) to make them thinner and alter other aspects of their bodies! I recommend you:
>
> - check the recommended age of games
> - read user reviews
> - assess the terms and conditions and privacy policy
> - avoid multi-player games where older children can upset your toddler or child when they play mean.

How much time a day is okay to play?

Until more studies are done it's very hard to know what the optimal number of minutes and hours of screen time might be. Professor Plowman states that there is no current hard evidence that access to devices causes harm. When thinking about how much time your toddler can play, there are so many factors to consider including your toddler's temperament and needs, and your family situation. Have the confidence to be firm with your toddler about how much time is okay, and be consistent; don't cave in if she pesters as then the amount of time she plays may just creep up and up.

If you focus on sharing the time that your toddler uses a device then you will be less likely to let your toddler overuse the devices. Tempting as it may be, try not to use devices as 'babysitting' tools.

As highlighted in other chapters in the book, your toddler should have no time on devices or television in the two hours before bed. This is because the blue light emitted from tablets, laptops and smartphones is disruptive to your toddler's circadian rhythms and sleep patterns.

In addition, I feel that toddlers, whatever the weather, need to have some time outdoors every day, so try to make sure that your toddler has a good balance of activities, strongly in favour of outside play and sharing books, with a short session playing with one app during the day.

Playing on smartphones and tablets needs to be a small part of a big life where toddlers should be playing and socialising in the real world. That means lots of opportunity to:

- dress up real dolls (with all of the dexterity that requires)
- real baking (with the mess, delayed gratification, and cakes that can truly be eaten and enjoyed)
- mark-making, drawing and painting on a variety of surfaces
- playing with and looking after real pets.

Whilst playing on a tablet is not passive like watching television, some of the guidelines that I would suggest are the same. So, I would recommend no technology:

- when your toddler is eating (for either of you!) as this is a great time to chat
- in their sleep space or bedroom so they do not see the blue-emitting lights at bedtime (which suppress melatonin production).

We should strive to make technology an asset to our family life and our toddler's development. This is much easier said than done but if we use our common sense we should be able to let technology be a positive force and not something that is snuffing out our connections with nature, the physical world and other people.

Is watching television okay for toddlers?

Broadcast television has changed out of all recognition from when I was a toddler. In most people's homes today it is possible to instantly find and select a television programme that your toddler will like to watch from children's programming, family films and cartoons. It can be very tempting to take advantage of this wall-to-wall access, so if you need to get something done or you want them to sit still and eat – TV, the ultimate convenient babysitter, is there ready and waiting. I say this not as disapproving 'expert' but as a parent who has also struggled in my relationship with toddler TV.

Several scientific studies of children have reported that too much television and media can lead to increased levels of attention problems, problems in school, sleep disturbance, obesity and other eating disorders.

The American Academy of Pediatrics (AAP) came out in 2011 with a stark recommendation that babies and toddlers under the age of two should not watch any television. This was a 'better safe than sorry' recommendation and they said, 'Until more research is done about the effects of TV on very young children, the American Academy of Pediatrics (AAP) does not recommend television for children age 2 or younger.'

This was a conclusion based on the fact that a child's brain develops rapidly during these first critical years. Interacting with other people and physical play is better for optimal development than television. For children older than two years, the AAP recommends no more than 1–2 hours per day of what they term 'high-quality' content. These include programmes that have been designed with child development in mind such as *In The Night Garden* and *Something Special.*

It is important to be firm with yourself and your toddler when it comes to screen time. If the rules are specific it makes it easier to enforce, and much easier for your toddler to accept them.

So, my suggestions would be:

- no televisions in bedrooms
- no television two hours before bedtime
- no watching television during meals (try to get into the habit of your children eating at a table)
- watch programmes with parents to make it a shared experience
- stick to television programmes that are well-made and designed for younger viewers with low edit cuts and lots of audience participation, e.g. *Mr Tumble*
- don't use television as either a reward or punishment
- try to schedule in family activities to entertain you all instead of television such as a game of cards or a walk after dinner.

How much television do you watch?

As a parent of a toddler you probably feel like flopping in front of the television after a long day or after an exhausting outing. However, it's worth remembering that toddlers look to their parents and model your behaviour. The good news is that having a toddler around is the perfect time to reassess some of our own bad habits. Some bad television habits that you might want to rethink include:

- having the television on all day as background noise
- ignoring your toddler's needs because you want to get through a box set. Yes they are addictive ... try to be strong!

- having loud, adult television programmes on when your toddler is up and about
- having a television in your room (sleep scientists say it is better for your sleep and cognitive functioning to keep all bedrooms television-free)
- endless channel surfing instead of planned viewing. Sitting together to watch a favourite film of the final of a baking or cookery show is a fun, shared experience.

real parent story

Katie (Ivan, 4 years)

'The iPad was a bit of a life saver for both me and Ivan. It is what reassured me that he had good cognitive development when he wasn't speaking or communicating. Some of the apps also gave me ideas for games to play with him so that we could communicate together.'

toddler health

'A little dirt doesn't hurt.'

American proverb

Our species has been fighting an ongoing arms race with bacteria, fungi, viruses and parasites for thousands of years. As a result, we have a highly developed immune system that protects us from invasion via our skin, gut and every orifice.

The importance of the symbiotic relationship between our bodies and the life that lives in them and on them is being revealed year-on-year. Our bodies contain more bacteria than human cells and this has huge health implications.

Genomic sequencing studies have reported that having high levels of 'bad flora' (pathological microbes) in our gut is correlated with increased prevalence of many illnesses and disorders including depression, allergies and autism. It is important to remember that correlation does not imply causation, that is to say, we cannot conclude that a high population of bad gut flora causes depression. However, there is a growing consensus in the medical profession that our health and well-being is inextricably linked with the living things that share our lives.

This is never more important than our guts which in Western countries are now largely devoid of intestinal worms. You may think this is a wonderful accomplishment and in many ways I'd agree, especially after my daughter and I caught thread worms when she was a toddler. One word: itchy!

However, when worming tablets were widely given to children in Ecuador there was an immediate increase in asthma and eczema. Many epidemiologists tried to understand what was happening, and the 'hygiene hypothesis' was born. The hygiene hypothesis suggests that when you remove too many parasites and microbes from the environment, our highly developed and active immune systems turn on our bodies and innocuous items and treat them like dangerous germs. So tiny floating pollen invokes a huge antihistamine response and hay fever is epidemic. Antibodies start to attack organs in the body leading to autoimmune diseases such as alopecia (where the body's antibodies attack all the hair follicles, killing them and leaving the person hairless). Even Type I diabetes is autoimmune at its core, with antibodies attacking and killing the pancreas.

That is not to say that the hygiene hypothesis explains all the increases in these diseases that we see. There is evidence that hormonal-disrupting chemicals and pollution produced by industry may explain increased levels of these diseases in developed countries too.

Boosting your toddler's immune system

So armed with this knowledge, what can we do? It is important that the world your toddler explores isn't 100 per cent germ-free. If your toddler has a healthy immune system and no underlying health problems you should be letting him get dirty, play with soil and worms, and not have endless baths and pristine clothes.

My advice to parents of toddlers without autoimmune diseases would be to embrace the natural microbes in the environment to boost friendly gut flora. Obviously handwashing before eating, and avoiding animal faeces go without saying!

It takes around six years for your child's immune system to mature. Below are some other ways in which you can support your toddler's immune system:

IMMUNISATIONS

Parents today are lucky not to live in a time where infectious diseases caused high levels of infant and toddler mortality. This is partly due to improved sanitisation but also undoubtedly due to childhood immunisation programmes that provide protection to individuals and communities from infectious diseases like measles, smallpox and polio. My children were always fully immunised with the vaccinations available on the NHS. This was particularly important for my eldest daughter who had a rare immune disease, as even secondary bacterial infections from chicken pox blisters could have potentially killed her.

FRUIT AND VEGETABLES

Offer your toddler plenty of fresh fruit and vegetables that contain antioxidants and other immune-boosting vitamins and minerals.

PROTEIN

Proteins are made up of amino acids that form the building blocks of the cells that form the immune system (and all cells!). The way the immune system fights germs is by increasing its own number, and to do this, it needs protein. So your toddler needs to eat protein-rich foods such as red meat, chicken, fish, eggs, lentils and other pulses.

CUT OUT THE SUGAR

Many studies have shown that a high-sugar diet, particularly highly processed, sugar-filled sweets and ready meals, suppresses the immune system, and may promote the growth of 'bad' bacteria in the gut. So keep your toddler's intake of sugar to a minimum to make sure he's in a good state to fight off germs. Fruit is a lovely sweet thing to eat.

SMOKE-FREE

The toxins in cigarette smoke have dangerous effects on all people, from the womb to adulthood. Keep your toddler away from cigarette smoke; this includes not smoking near him, but also avoid cigarette smoke on your clothes and furniture. Exposure to cigarette smoke increases the risk of bronchitis, asthma and ear infections in toddlers – chronic illnesses like asthma can weaken your toddler's immune system. If you or your partner still smoke, speak to the NHS helpline for support with giving up smoking. If you still smoke, do not smoke in the home, and after each cigarette wash your face and hands. Ideally change your clothes when you come back inside. Do not smoke with your toddler in the car, either.

Vitamin D deficiency

Life in the UK today involves lots of time indoors, lots of time covered in clothes, and when we have good weather we wear high-factor sunscreen. This has led to an epidemic in vitamin D deficiency.

Studies have reported vitamin D deficiency is associated with increased risk of many chronic disorders, including cancer, multiple sclerosis, type II diabetes and cardiovascular, autoimmune and neurological diseases.

We cannot get sufficient vitamin D from our diets as vitamin D is not really a vitamin at all, but a hormone manufactured in our skin when it is exposed to sunlight. Vitamin D is important as it regulates genes that control cell growth and development, immune function and metabolic control. Groups like the Royal College of Paediatrics and Child Health are so concerned about modern levels of vitamin D deficiency in pregnant women, babies, toddlers and children that they are recommending vitamin D supplementation.

There are a number of ways that you can make sure that your toddler gets enough vitamin D and the first is good old-fashioned sunshine. Getting outside is really important for your toddler. As well as vitamin D production, sunshine and fresh air has all-round benefits for your toddler's sleep, fitness and mental well-being.

In the UK it is impossible to manufacture enough vitamin D in the skin between the colder months from October to March. This means you need to give your toddler a vitamin D supplement in these months. This is especially important if your toddler is covered up a lot because he has fair skin, wears lots of clothes for cultural reasons, or if he has very dark skin. Skin should never be allowed to burn, but around 15 minutes of sun exposure between 11am and 4pm produces enough vitamin D. If this is not possible you will need to rely on vitamin D drops.

Using antibiotics

Asking your doctor to prescribe antibiotics every time your toddler has an upper respiratory tract infection is not good for your child or the population at large. Most of the time these infections are viral and antibiotics don't kill viruses.

The UK is now much stricter about prescribing antibiotics, but sadly, many other countries still have doctors who prescribe them all the time and even as a preventative measure.

The downside of overuse of antibiotics in recent history has meant that sometimes toddlers with serious bacterial sepsis do not get antibiotics as soon as they need them. Doctors trying to reduce the amounts of antibiotics that are prescribed may wrongly diagnose a bacterial infection as a viral infection. Make sure as a parent you are aware of the signs of meningitis and sepsis (see below) and that you seek urgent medical attention if you feel that your toddler is seriously ill.

DID YOU KNOW?

In 1928 British scientist Alexander Fleming working in his lab in St Mary's Hospital in London discovered that Penicillium mould killed Staphylococcus aureus bacteria. He concluded that the mould produced a substance that kept the bacteria at bay – he called this first antibiotic penicillin.

In the 1940s scientists began trying to manufacture penicillin and this naturally occurring antibiotic killed many bacterial infections because these bacteria had never before been exposed to the Penicillium mould, and they were practically powerless against the penicillin it produced. This was such a monumental discovery in a time when death by infectious disease was still common and for this research Alexander Fleming won the Nobel Prize in Physiology and Medicine.

Managing a fever

A fever is a high temperature over 37.5°C (99.5°F). In order to check your toddler's temperature I recommend a digital ear thermometer (you can even use it at night when your toddler is asleep).

Although as a parent it can be very worrying if your child has a high temperature, fevers are quite common in the toddler years. They are often a response to a viral infection which often clears up by itself without treatment. Fevers are often treated like a fire that must be put out by parents. This stems from a basic misunderstanding about what a fever is. A fever is an adaptation *by the body* to kill an invading infection, be it a bacteria or a virus. Fevers are particularly effective at killing viruses as viruses struggle to replicate and infect a host if the body temperature rises above a certain temperature.

If your child is feverish, keep him hydrated, as he can lose lots of water through sweating. There is no need to actively bring down a fever with fans or cold baths; this may confuse your toddler's brain into driving up his body temperature even further.

To help reduce your toddler's temperature you can:

- keep him dressed in cool, light cotton clothes
- use a lightweight cotton sheet instead of a sleeping bag or duvet
- keep his room cool at around 18°C
- give him children's paracetamol or ibuprofen. These medicines are also painkillers. Antipyretics (fever reducing medicines) aren't always necessary. Ask your pharmacist for advice.

Sometimes high fevers in toddlers are associated with more serious signs and symptoms, such as:

- respiratory distress – look for ribs sucking in, fast breathing, pale or blue lips, the 'tug' of air being sucked in at the throat, belly breathing – basically any evidence that your toddler is really struggling to get enough oxygen. This is an emergency and you should call 999
- vomiting and diarrhoea
- non-blanching rash (look to gums and soles of feet if your toddler has dark skin)
- fits or seizures.

Serious bacterial illnesses associated with fevers include:

- bacterial meningitis – infection of the meninges (the protective membranes that surround the brain and spinal cord)
- sepsis or septicaemia – infection of the blood
- urinary tract infection (UTI) or kidney infection
- pneumonia – infected and inflamed lungs.

Whilst I prefer to allow my children to maintain a mild fever when they are fighting an infection, it is important to realise that fevers in themselves can be dangerous to children if they get too high. Unchecked temperatures can lead to febrile seizures which can be very frightening for parents to see:

- your toddler's body will be stiff with twitching arms and legs for five minutes or less
- he will be unconscious and unresponsive during the seizure
- he may wet or soil himself
- his eyes might roll back, he may vomit or produce froth in his mouth
- afterwards, your toddler may be sleepy for at least an hour.

Febrile seizures are frightening but most children make a complete recovery afterwards. If your toddler has a febrile seizure, follow the following steps:

- place your toddler in the recovery position by lying him on his side with one cheek on the floor. Having his face turned to one side keeps his airway open
- stay with your toddler and time how long the febrile seizure lasts
- if a first seizure or it lasts longer than five minutes, call 999 for an ambulance or get to hospital
- if not a first seizure or it lasts less than five minutes, call 111 for emergency advice
- after the seizure take off any extra clothing to help cool down your toddler's temperature
- don't put anything in your toddler's mouth.

Meningitis or sepsis

Children and adults (including a friend of mine) die needlessly from undiagnosed meningococcal meningitis or sepsis every year. It's really important to know the signs of this potentially fatal condition in toddlers. If you see these symptoms, don't take a chance, and seek emergency medical assessment and treatment immediately. Signs and symptoms of meningococcal meningitis or sepsis in toddlers include:

- a high fever, with cold hands and feet
- mottled legs with poor circulation
- vomiting
- refusing to eat
- agitated or delirious and not wanting to be picked up
- drowsy, floppy and unresponsive
- rapid breathing and sometimes grunting
- pale, blotchy skin
- a dark red, non-blanching rash that doesn't fade when a glass is rolled over it
- a stiff neck
- dislike of bright lights
- convulsions or seizures.

Don't wait for all these symptoms and don't wait for the famous rash. These symptoms might appear in any order and some may not appear at all.

A study of casualty departments reported that the best predictor of how severe a child's illness was was not the triage assessment by medical staff but how worried the parents were. So trust your instincts and if your toddler is 'not right' get urgent medical assessment.

Toddler teeth

By the time your toddler is a year old he will have several beautiful pearly white milk teeth. Even though these are his deciduous milk teeth, it's important to look after them:

- clean his teeth twice a day (he will need help until he is at least eight years old). If your toddler is resistant to you cleaning his teeth you could negotiate a situation where he is allowed to do the first clean (or the last clean) and you get to clean as well for a total of around two minutes. Be really gentle as it can be very uncomfortable and painful having someone else clean your teeth. You can use toothbrushes that light up for two minutes, or an egg timer, to help him see how long to clean his teeth. Another technique is to tell him a story or sing a song while you clean

- choose water or milk for his main drinks – fruit juice can cause tooth decay and fizzy drinks are not appropriate for children
- the Department of Health recommends fluoride toothpaste, but make sure that your toddler doesn't swallow it. Use a pea-sized amount only
- use a small toddler's toothbrush to clean each tooth in very small circles
- register with an NHS dentist and book your toddler in for a check-up every six months. Dental care is free for children up to the age of 18 (if in full-time education)
- save treats containing sugar to be eaten after a main meal
- do not brush your toddler's teeth straight after a meal as it weakens the enamel; wait for at least half an hour
- change your toddler's toothbrush when the bristles start to look messy and curve outwards
- avoid food and sugary drinks before bedtime
- don't put anything other than milk in a bottle as this can lead to tooth decay. Graduate your toddler onto a Sippy cup if he hasn't learned to use one already
- try to change snacks to less sugary ones. Raisins, for example, are very popular but they get stuck in your toddler's molars.

TIP BOX: LEARN SOME BASIC FIRST AID

Look out for a first aid course; some health visitor centres and GP surgeries offer them. Companies such as St John's Ambulance also offer courses aimed specifically at young families.

real parent story

Katrina (Andrew, 13 months)

'I did a first aid course at our community centre. It was just a short, basic course but when Andrew was choking once I immediately began performing back slaps with him lying down across my legs. He brought up this huge ball of fluff that he'd been picking up off the floor. It was such a relief to be able to save him, I can't imagine how awful it would have been not to know what to do.'

TOP TIP

Never worry that doctors, health visitors or A&E will be angry or irritated that you have brought your toddler to them for assessment. All good healthcare professionals will respect a parent's gut feeling that their child is unwell. Toddlers can become very ill, very quickly, so it's always better to get him checked out quickly than stay at home stressed and risking his health

TOP TIP

There is a growing swell of evidence of the importance of the health of our digestive system, namely that we develop healthy gut bacteria. I wish I had been better at encouraging my children to eat probiotic yoghurt and to avoid too much sugar (which helps promote the growth of so-called 'bad' bacteria in the gut). It is possible to buy probiotic sachets that can build the good bacteria in your toddler's gut which may have far-reaching implications for their health.

Final thoughts

I hope that *The Calm and Happy Toddler* has reassured you of your unique ability to watch, understand and nurture your child through her toddler years. Parents are under so much scrutiny today, and I think that the vast majority of parents are just such wonderful examples of the power of unconditional love.

Toddlerhood is such an intense time for both the toddler and her parents. She is learning to talk, move independently and exert her will on the world. This metamorphosis takes just a short time in the life of a person, and yet so much happens. Try to enjoy the rollercoaster, and remember 'everything is a phase'.

As your child moves into her preschool years you will once again get to enjoy a new stage, with new challenges and new wonderful experiences. I particularly love the conversations that you can begin to have with your pre-schooler child – they really are budding philosophers at this age. Before that I hope you will enjoy my list of suggested things to do with your toddler – like a little plastic bucket list of things that I really enjoyed doing with my toddlers at the time.

I wish you well as your child leaves the toddler years and applaud you for doing such a great job of loving her, playing with her and being her secure base. A loving parent like you really allows a child to build firm foundations for the future, and parents are fundamental in developing happy, healthy, loving and loved people.

appendix

50 things to try before your toddler is 3¾

'The bitter tears shed over graves are for words left unsaid and deeds left undone.'

Harriet Beecher Stowe

In homage to The National Trust's brilliant *100 things to do before you are 11¾* campaign to get children enjoying an active life, I present my guide to 50 things you can do with your toddler before he turns 3¾.

This list is supposed to be fun and inspiring, to give you a few ideas, so please treat it that way rather than as a list of 'must-dos'. If your toddler has learning difficulties or hearing difficulties he may race through the physical list and not be ready for the social list until he is older. Some of these will need a bit of discreet supervision, of course, but try to let your child have a go on his own, where possible. I'd also love your suggestions so the list can get better over time and become a community project. So if you have a suggestion please get in touch on my community Facebook page at: www.facebook.com/calmandhappytoddler

Physical experiences

1. Walking barefoot in mud
2. Swimming with your toddler on your back
3. Paddling at the seaside
4. Riding a pony
5. Go down a giant inflatable slide
6. Learn to push self on a swing by leaning forwards and backwards

7. Throw stick for a dog
8. Learn to catch
9. Kick a ball
10. Pick up a worm or a snail
11. Clamber on the lower branches of a tree
12. Collect wild blackberries (and wild blueberries if you are lucky to get the chance)
13. Ride a scooter
14. Learn to balance on a balance bike
15. Learn a dance of any style you like: pop, street dance, folk dance, anything
16. Play on a pile of gravel
17. Play on a sand dune

Making experiences

18. Make tea for the fairies
19. Make rosewater perfume
20. Make blackberry crumble with foraged blackberries
21. Grow cress
22. Grow tomatoes
23. Grow herbs
24. Grow strawberries
25. Choose and paint a pebble from a river
26. Paint a pot or tile – without assistance
27. Make a bed for a favourite teddy

Thinking experiences

28. Sort socks into piles
29. Do a sinking and floating experiment
30. Water play with funnels and cups
31. Visit a farm or 'pick-your-own' to learn about food

Social experiences

32. Have a birthday party
33. Take a dog for a walk
34. Have a play date
35. Have a day with grandparents
36. Spend time with godparents
37. Build a den with a friend
38. Have a pretend tea party with teddies and maybe a friend
39. Hold a small animal like a rat, guinea pig or rabbit
40. Have a cake sale for charity on your street

Language experiences

41. Learn an action song
42. Tell your name to your parent's friend
43. Tell your age to a shopkeeper
44. Buy bread from a shop
45. Share a book with Mum or Dad every day
46. Order a babyccino in a café

Emotional experiences

47. Cuddle your parents every day
48. Kiss your parents every day
49. Stroke a cat
50. Tell Mum and Dad that you love them every day – and be told back

resources

Parents are bombarded with gurus, opinions and conflicting information on the Internet and beyond. Here is my list of go-to resources that I find expert and impartial or compelling and fun!

Health and Development

NHS CHOICES WEBSITE (WWW.NHS.UK)

Here you'll find Department of Health recommendations (which I have tried to include in this book where applicable). NHS Choices has a newsletter that you can sign up to that will send you texts or emails aimed at each age and stage of your toddler.

THE ESSENTIAL PARENT COMPANY (WWW.ESSENTIALPARENT.COM)

As one of the co-founders of the company along with my ex-colleagues from the BBC, we have produced lots of videos to help you see various things that are hard to read in books e.g., what a meningitis rash looks like and how to do the tumbler test.

Language

I CAN COMMUNICATION CHARITY (WWW.TALKINGPOINT.ORG.UK)

This is a brilliant parent and carer-facing website which is a great place to go to if you are concerned about your toddler's language or communication.

Facebook Following

I think Steve Biddulph is wonderful and I strongly recommend that you follow his Facebook community pages 'Raising Girls' and 'Raising Boys'.

Classic Texts

As a child development researcher who did my research at an attachment lab I have to list two old but timeless books:

Attachment by John Bowlby
The Expression of the Emotions in Man and Animals by Charles
    Darwin

Motherhood

My book is written for all parents but here are two books that beautifully explore what it means to become a Mum:

What Mothers Do: Especially When it Looks Like Nothing by
    Naomi Stadlen
The Seven Stages of Motherhood by Ann Pleshette Murphy

Funny

You really need to keep your sense of humour when you have a toddler! For this reason I recommend following these accounts on Twitter:

@HonestToddler
@HuffPostParents

Toddler Storybooks

Each Peach Pear Plum by Allan and Janet Ahlberg
Room on the Broom by Julia Donaldson
Green Eggs and Ham by Dr Seuss

acknowledgements

I would like to dedicate this book to my wonderful mum, Katrina. If anyone should be writing a book about toddlers it should be her. Not only did she have three toddlers of her own but she has been the most brilliant Grandma to her eight grandchildren as they toddled and waddled and learned to talk. She has been my secure base in this world and supported me throughout my studies and my interest in child development.

Special thanks also to my sister Katie, who has taught me so much about being a parent to a child with special needs. My adorable nephew Ivan is autistic and is blessed to have a warm, unflappable, resourceful, fun and deeply loving mum who is such an inspiration to me.

Thanks to the team at Vermilion: Sam Jackson, Julia Kellaway, Catherine Knight, Morwenna Loughman and Lucy Oates who have vastly improved the book and stretched me to write the best book I can.

Finally, my deepest thanks, love and gratitude to my family. To Rufus, my husband, who has looked after our children so that I could research and write this book in my spare time. Thanks and eternal love also to my very patient, wonderful children Miranda, Benedict and Iris; I am so privileged to be their mum. They were adorable babies and hilarious toddlers, and as they get older I just love being with them every day and treasure my memories of mothering them, teaching them and playing with them.

index